W

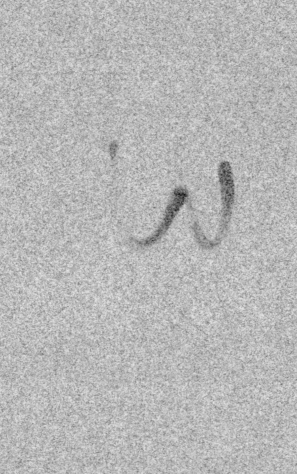

Suzuki

GSX-R750

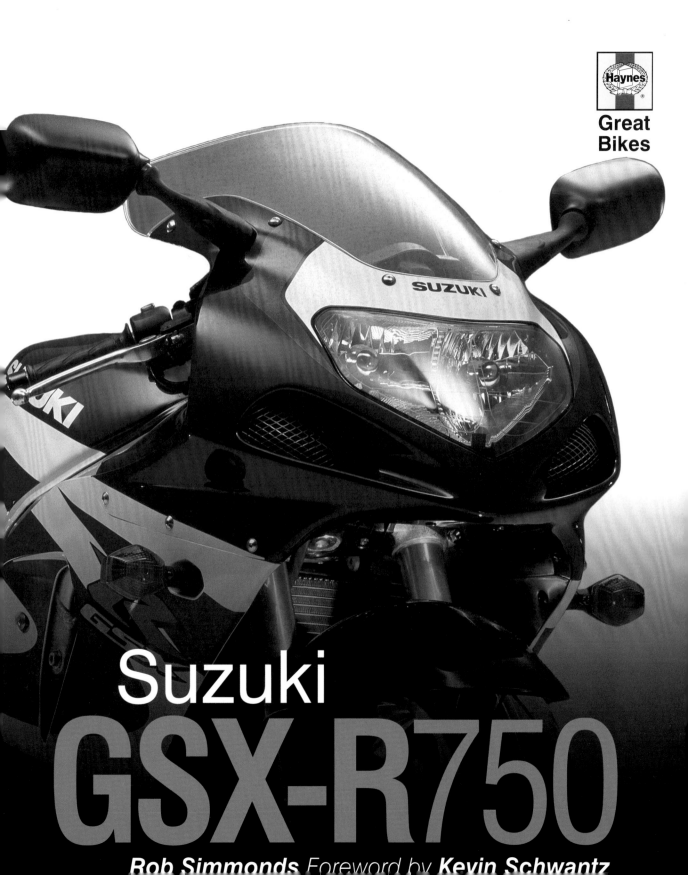

Great
Bikes

Suzuki
GSX-R750

Rob Simmonds *Foreword by* **Kevin Schwantz**

HAYNES GREAT BIKES **SUZUKI GSX-R750**

First published in 2002

British Library cataloguing-in-publication data:
A catalogue record for this book is available from the British Library.

Published by Haynes Publishing,
Sparkford, Yeovil, Somerset BA22 7JJ

Tel: 01963 440635 Fax: 01963 440001
Int. tel: +44 1963 440635 Int. fax: +44 1963 440001

E-mail: sales@haynes-manuals.co.uk
Web site: www.haynes.co.uk

ISBN 1 85960 821 3

Library of Congress catalog card number 2001099294

Haynes North America Inc.
861 Lawrence Drive, Newbury Park,
California 91320, USA

Printed and bound in Great Britain by J. H. Haynes & Co. Ltd

Contents

Acknowledgements

Many thanks to all who helped me while writing this book, including:

Kevin Schwantz for the foreword; Jamie Whitham, for giving of his vast GSX-R750 racing experience; and Nicolas Sauhet for helping source GSX-R750 brochures from France and helping with research – *Merci, mon ami*!

At *Bike Magazine*: Tim Thompson, for allowing me access to *Bike*'s archives; Martin Child, for his help on all things GSX-R; and special thanks to Hugo Wilson for his inspiration in the opening paragraph of the very first chapter.

At *Motor Cycle News*: Editor Rob McDonnell and all at the archives.

At *Two Wheels Only*: Everybody, including Gus Scott, Darren Scott, Dawn Brooks, Leonard Grant, Jim Bowen, 'Diddy' Daryll Young, John Cantlie, Alex Hearn, Mark Shippey, and Giles Butcher, for letting me panic in the office as I tried to hit the copy deadline for this book.

At *Suzuki UK*: Amy Heitman, Jason McLean, and Jenni Foulkes from Redcat Marketing Services.

Also, a big thanks to *Suzuki 2* magazine and Mountain Media Limited's Carole Bohanan and Graham Scott for help and meditation techniques.

Picture acknowledgements: Firstly, a massive thanks to Luke Brackenbury at *Bike* magazine for searching out some of the older shots used in this book. Cheers mate! Other photographers I would also like to thank are: Tim Kent for the cover shot; Don Morley for the early race shots; Mark Wernham for all the post-1992 race shots; Jason Critchell for some of the *Bike* mag shots; Phil Masters; and Roland Brown.

Finally, many thanks to Gary Pinchin and his superb book *Suzuki GSX-R750*, published by Crowood. It chronicles in depth the early racing successes of the GSX-R, especially its Endurance victories, and is well worth a read – as is *Kevin Schwantz – The World's Champion*, by Peter Clifford and Shirley Schwantz.

Foreword
by Kevin Schwantz

I still remember the first time I saw the Suzuki GSX-R750. I had been riding the GS700 in 1985, so to see this thing was amazing. We actually got it a year later in the States than in Europe, but it was like, WOW, that thing looks like a race bike! It was great to see the GSX-R come along when it did and it's been nice for me to see it develop over the years from 1985 onwards. In the right hands it has been a world-beater since it first came out.

Since then, the level of performance that production motorcycles like the GSX-R750 have gotten to is awesome. You can buy from your Suzuki dealer a motorcycle that is lighter and faster than my 1988 Daytona 200 winning machine. In just over ten years that is how far motorcycles have come. It has been a real treat to see the GSX-R develop, and to be part of its history.

As long as Suzuki make the GSX-R, I reckon I will always have a job!

Introduction

Without a doubt the Suzuki GSX-R was a landmark motorcycle. When it burst on to the scene at the end of 1984, it was just so different to all that had gone before. Here was a machine that looked and handled like a World TTF1 race machine, yet you could go and buy it in the shops.

Since then, every sportsbike built owes a debt of gratitude to it, for starting a class of motorcycles that is one of the most popular in the world. Whatever sports machine you ride, it all started with the GSX-R750.

But even that's not the full story of this amazing machine. While its peers slipped by the wayside, Suzuki continued to develop the GSX-R750, and 17 years after its launch it and its family members are still going strong.

Even with all that weight over the front end, he still can't keep the front wheel on the ground. The author on a GSX-RW.
(Mark Wernham)

The race heritage of the first GSX-R750 is evident in this brochure shot. (Suzuki)

In the beginning...

Numbers are vitally important when it comes to motorcycles.

Numbers equate to power, and weight (or the lack of it). They also indicate the price of a machine, and how much it will cost to insure. Numbers can show how the bike steers, how the bike performs.

But perhaps most importantly, numbers show the capacity of the motorcycle, usually emblazoned somewhere along its side. To see the right number on the side of a fairing is like wearing the right designer label or proper brand of trainers. For many years, the number '750' has been important in motorcycling. In the 1960s and 1970s it was Honda's landmark CB750 that wore it, alongside BSA and Triumph triples. Epoch-marking machines like the Ducati 750SS also wore this number proudly, along with the manic two-stroke triples from Kawasaki and Suzuki.

The number and capacity of 750 have always been special, and in the 1980s one particular machine marked another, very important rebirth of the 750cc category. If you were into this sort of two-wheeled numbers game, then the 1984 Cologne show must have been a wonderful place to be.

A new machine from Suzuki made its debut at Cologne that year. It had two big bug eyes and a minimalist slab-sided beauty. In a world of mid-1980s flabby excessiveness, it was a stripped-to-the-waist fighter. Little wonder, then, that it could boast a direct lineage from Suzuki racers past such as the 1977 GS750, the 1978 GS1000, the 1980 GS1000R, and the 1984 GSX750.

The GSX-R wasn't the only new 750cc four-stroke to debut at the Cologne show, or even the only 'hot' machine to come from Suzuki or anyone else that very year. Yamaha was also making its presence felt with a liquid-cooled inline four called the FZ750. The main catalyst for this particular capacity's popularity was simple: racing's premier four-stroke classes – Formula One and Endurance racing – were moving from 1,000cc to 750cc. And these two machines, the GSX-R and FZ750, were set against each other in a bid for glory, both in the showrooms and on track. Meanwhile, Suzuki was aiming a two-stroke race replica at the streets too, with a square-four 500cc GP refugee, the RG500. Honda was also out in force with their new stroker, the NS400R, while Kawasaki were re-inventing the 600 class with the sporty GPZ600R.

Dealing with the 750s, Suzuki with the GSX-R and Yamaha with the FZ were both ground-breaking in their own way. The Yamaha was ground-breaking in a technological sense. Internally, its heart was blessed with five valves per cylinder – three inlet and two exhaust – and also water cooling. In comparison, the Suzuki's

real innovation came from the whole styling exercise of the bike and its utter minimalism. Here was a bike that looked like it had fallen off the back of a race transporter, but was actually a high-volume production machine. It had four valves per cylinder, not five. Oil and air cooling, not liquid. It even had a little less power than the FZ. But it was that racing heritage and look which would ensure that the GSX-R would outlive both the FZ and its own two-stroke RG brother.

In the late 1970s, both Suzuki and Kawasaki began to launch attacks on Honda's dominant stranglehold of the World Endurance series. In 1980 Suzuki won three rounds of the series – including the Bol d'Or, at their first attempt – and these successes gave the factory the impetus it needed to develop more effective machines with which to attack the opposition. Early in 1981 rumours began to emerge of a new endurance racer from Suzuki, boasting an aluminium alloy frame and 997cc four-stroke motor. Reports put the top speed of this new machine at around 175mph (282kph), which it was reputed to have reached on one of Suzuki's own test tracks. The use of aluminium for such machines was in its infancy, although many privateers were experimenting with frames made from similar light alloys.

This bike was called the GS1000R or XR41, and although early development machines featured twin shocks like the earlier steel-framed XR69 rather than a monoshock unit, the XR41 is now accepted as being the father of the GSX-R750. For the next two years Suzuki continually developed the XR41, while Kawasaki and Serge Rosset's prepared K1000J racers took the 1981 and 1982 World Endurance titles. This development work paid off for the Suzuki factory in 1983, when the XR41, backed by HB, managed by Dominique Meliand, and ridden by the enigmatic Frenchman Herve Moineau and Belgian Richard Hubin, took the World Endurance title – the last which would be fought

between 1,000cc inline fours for the best part of the next 20 years. The following year saw a change in the rules limiting capacity to 750cc, so Suzuki saw plenty of mileage in a machine based on their racing pedigree with the XR41, but with a 750cc inline four-cylinder motor. Suzuki would look upon the road bike resulting from the marriage of the XR41 chassis and 750cc motor as a production racer first and a road bike second.

In charge of the project was Etsuo Yokouchi, with Yasunobo Fujii looking after the engine and Takayoshi Suzuki the chassis. Yokouchi was a good choice to lead the team. He was a strong supporter of Suzuki's racing programme, being the race team manager for 1983, and was an advocate of the production of high performance motorcycles (especially after visiting European racetracks and asking what type of bike riders wanted), as well as having a reputation for demanding perfection from those around him and rejecting design details that didn't meet his very high standards.

In Suzuki's in-house magazine *Tech News*, Yokouchi reasoned that as the class-leading GSX-R400 was 19 per cent lighter than its competitors, its 750 brother should aim for a similar saving of, say, 20 per cent. With 750s of the time coming in at around 220kg (485lb) this gave the target weight of the new Suzuki as 176kg (388lb). Engine man Fujii-san therefore had a target for him and his team to reach. They had to make an engine which was as light as possible to help in this weight-saving, and also hit around 100PS, which is equivalent to 100bhp or about 74.6kW. Extensive use of computers and finite element analysis would help find ways of reducing friction in the engine and cutting weight, but it would be convention – as well as Suzuki's recent expertise – which would decide the basic layout of the motor. The GSX-R750 engine was to be an inline four-cylinder with four valves per cylinder.

One of the major problems encountered by

Fujii and his engineers was that of cooling. With the amount of power needed for so little weight, Fujii couldn't have the luxury of water cooling with its associated jacket and piping. Ironically, water cooling would find its way on to the GSX-R750 seven years later, but at the time Suzuki personnel considered that oil/air cooling was the best available option. The solution was found in the licence-built Packard Merlin engines used on the North American P51 Mustang fighter aircraft. When discussing cooling properties, Fujii and his team often looked at aero piston engines. They found that the Packard Merlin – an American-licensed copy of the Rolls-Royce Merlin engine (which also powered the classic Spitfire and Hurricane fighters) – used a novel way of cooling itself. In addition to liquid cooling it used a spray of oil, which squirted from jets onto the undersides of the piston crowns.

This system was replicated and adapted for use on the GSX-R, which necessitated the use of two oil pumps. The first did the normal job of lubricating crankshaft bearings, the forked rocker arm assemblies, and the camshafts, as well as squirting oil onto the underside of the pistons. The remainder of the heat generated at the top end was drawn away from the hot spots and back to the sump by oil from pump number two. This secondary supply of oil was pumped under pressure to a gallery in the large magnesium head (a head made of this lightweight material was a first in 1985), which was finned for quicker heat dissipation. From here it was squirted down onto the outside surface of the combustion chambers through eight oil channels. Once it had done its job it drained back to the sump through the central cam chain tunnel.

As the oil did a big job in the heart of the motor, Suzuki placed a large capacity oil cooler on the GSX-R750, along with a fan which was thermostatically operated. Suzuki claimed the cooling system had a capacity four times that of conventional coolers. The whole system received

the acronym SACS, which stood for Suzuki Advanced Cooling System – despite the fact that one of the ideas behind it came from an antique warbird! Cooler operating temperatures meant that some significant parts of the engine could be made lighter, which in turn made for a revvier and more powerful unit as well as a reduction in overall weight.

Compared to the previous Suzuki GSX750 (GSX700 in the USA) the crankshaft journals and overall crank diameter were reduced in size, and con-rods, pistons, and gudgeon pins were also much lighter than on the air-cooled GSX. Fujii and his team were able to shave a further kilo (2.2lb) from the whole plot by casting the cylinder head cover in magnesium. Suzuki's TSCC (Twin Swirl Combustion Chamber) also featured improvements for use in the new GSX-R750. Inlet valves were increased to 26mm and exhaust increased to 23mm, and the chamber itself was redesigned. Similarly to the Kawasaki GPZ900R, the Suzuki used perfectly straight inlet tracts for improved efficiency. Breathing through race-type 29mm flat-slide carburettors, peak power was 100bhp (74.6kW) at 10,500rpm, with maximum torque of 52.1lb ft (70.65Nm) at 9,000rpm. In comparison, the Yamaha FZ750 made 57.9lb ft (78.51Nm) at just 8,000 revs.

The end result was an engine that provided a lot of power for little weight. Like many Suzuki engines before and since, this motor was tough. Suzuki engineers destruction tested one motor at 12,500rpm for 30 hours and yet it was still in one piece at the end! The fact that you were riding a bike with a peaky, race-orientated engine was also clear when you looked at the tacho, which only *began* at 3,000 revs. Power from the engine was transmitted through a six-speed gearbox and a hydraulic clutch.

If poor Fujii-san had it tough, then at least he had a shoulder to cry on. The unenviable task of paring the frame and all its attached components to the bone was given to Takayoshi Suzuki, and

Compared to the machines of the day, the GSX-R750 engine was powerful and compact. (Suzuki)

with most of the considerable 44kg (96.8lb) weight saving coming from the chassis perhaps he was the man with the harder job. Suzuki's *Tech News* revealed how hard this weight saving – which must have bordered on the obsessive – was: 'Try to imagine the polite but rather intense discussions between engine design team chief and the chassis design team chief, concerning exactly where to shave 44 kilos (96.8lb) off the overall weight of the GSX-R750 with Mr. Yokouchi looking over both their shoulders.'

This obsession for weight loss and utter scrutiny to the Nth degree of parts and components always marks out a special machine. History would repeat itself not just with successive GSX-R models, but with machines that lay in the future, such as the Honda FireBlade, Yamaha YZF-R1, and Suzuki's own GSX-R1000.

Suzuki had been at the forefront of aluminium chassis design with machines like the 1983 RG250 – perhaps the first true 'race-replica' for

MCN's Mat Oxley on the 750F at Ryuyo. (*Bike/MCN*)

the road – and the firm's previous 750, the GSX.
Scrutinising these chassis, they found that the
best way to cut down on chassis and frame
weight was to make them much more simply.
This meant cutting down on the number of
components and even on the number of welds.
The GSX750 had what was probably the first
mass-produced aluminium alloy frame on a bike

and it had a total of 96 components. For the
GSX-R750 the target was just 32 components,
and eventually Suzuki-san and his team got this
figure down to 26, utilising five cold-cast
aluminium alloy components and 21 pieces of
extruded aluminium. More weight was saved by
using lightweight rivets from the aerospace
industry. Ultimately, the completed frame

weighed in at just 8.1kg (17.8lb), which was less than half as much as a conventional steel frame of the time.

To ape a race bike, the suspension on the new GSX-R750 had to be of excellent quality. The skinny 37mm diameter forks used on the previous GSX750 were replaced by beefier 41mm items. The triple clamps holding everything in place were also now made of aluminium and were bigger than before. The forks featured Suzuki's New Electronically Activated Suspension (NEAS) Positive Damping Fork (PDF), which was fitted in a bid to stop the forks diving so much under hard braking. This system was activated by the initial application of the brakes. This in turn would restrict the movement of oil in the forks, which effectively eliminated much of the 'dive'. The forks also included four-way adjustability. Despite making everything thicker and stronger, the use of aluminium actually meant that the front-end was lighter than the old GSX. The Full Floater rear suspension used on the GSX-R reportedly featured 35 per cent less parts than previous incarnations and was much more compact and yet stronger. In the damping, Suzuki incorporated an eccentric cam which made the bike much less harsh and therefore more comfortable at maximum extension and yet gave a firmer ride at maximum compression, hopefully giving the rider the best of both worlds – comfort when going steady under load, and sports suspension when really going for it.

Wheels were, curiously, 18-inch items front and rear, which was a little strange as the rest of the world favoured the quicker-steering attributes of 16-inch wheels on road bikes. Still, at the time Suzuki's endurance racers were wearing exactly the same, and these offered faster wheel changes during pit stops and would mean the tyres would last longer. Brakes were new Dual Opposed Piston (DOP, yet

another acronym from Suzuki) four-piston calipers, grasping 300mm race-like drilled steel discs.

The mimicry of the race bike extended not just to components and performance, but to styling and ergonomics as well, and one glance at the GSX-R750 told you it was a racer. At the front you have those huge, bug-eye endurance-style headlights and full fairing, through which you can just make out the minimalism of the engine and the unique signature of that double cradle frame, atop which sits the flat-topped endurance-style tank. At the back the tail unit hugs the closest line to the subframe and features two scalloped seats and even a grab rail. On the paintwork side of things, the use of the Suzuki corporate two blues and white is breathtaking, and the huge 'R' on the tank and fairing confirmed in no uncertain terms that this was a racer. Still, if you did miss that, then on the tank was emblazoned 'Hyper Sports', just to make sure you knew what you were getting into. And the view from the seat was just that. Like a good suit, you *wore* the GSX-R750. The ergonomics of the GS1000R XR41 were faithfully replicated, so you bolted yourself into the race experience.

It was a bold move from Suzuki, to take all the elements of a race bike and put it on to the road. To illustrate to potential customers just what sort of machine the GSX-R750 was, the brochure cover was shot at Paul Ricard with one of the endurance racers in the background, and the phrase 'born on the circuit and returned to the circuit' was used in the literature. With such a race-bike-like look came an amazingly speedy development time. Engineers spent most of 1983 discussing the project before getting the go-ahead in January 1984. In May of that year a prototype was spotted at Suzuki's Ryuyo test track, and the finished machine was on display at the Cologne show that October. It was a remarkable speed at which to develop such a revolutionary bike. But was the world ready for it?

Press response to the GSX-R750

As usual, it was the UK's *Motor Cycle News* which was first with the low-down on the GSX-R, a machine which would spark off a whole new trend towards road bikes aping their racetrack brethren. A young Mat Oxley – himself a respected endurance racer and TT winner – found that the new Suzuki was simply stunning when he got to ride it for the first time in January 1985 at Suzuki's Ryuyo test track. He wrote: 'The Japanese have finally realised that compromise needn't dictate sportsbike design. Suzuki's new GSX-R750 is closer to a four-stroke racer on the road than anything else before. It is to the F1 racer as the RD500LC is to the GP machine. The two design goals of 100bhp and 388lb made it impossible for Suzuki's engineers to compromise – even if they wanted to. At Suzuki's test track the machine blatantly betrayed its racetrack development. Like a real racing bike, the GSX-R responds to a hard rider and has its own idiosyncrasies that make it more like a machine straight from the racetrack.'

MCN's test hinted that this was a machine with giant-killing ability under its fairing, thanks to that light weight and high power. 'The engine is pure racer,' said Oxley, 'with that raw edge that distinguishes the genuine from the pretend. Power is at its best from 7,000rpm to the 11,000

Like a prize fighter stripped to the waist, the GSX-R looked more aggressive with its clothes off. (Suzuki)

Another cutaway of the engine, this time from the other side.
(Suzuki)

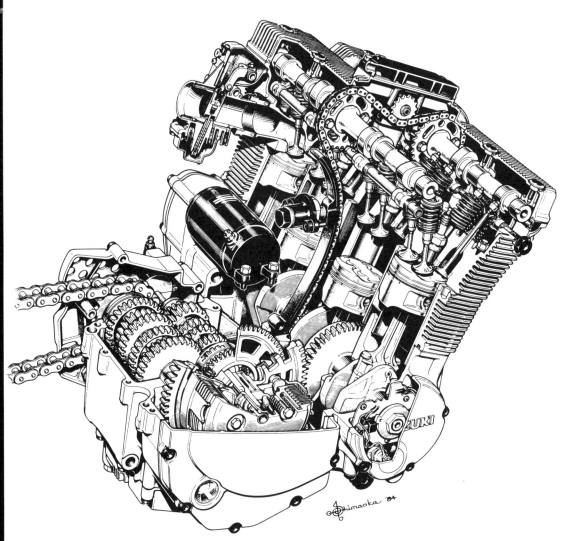

redline. Within that range the GSX-R will see off many 1,000s, but it does so at the expense of some mid-range torque.'

Superbike's Graham Scott wrote: 'The GSX-R750 is, according to some people, essentially the most remarkable achievement since splitting the atom. That oil-cooled motor is light and very powerful. It will pull from the 3,000rpm baseline, is fairly flat until 6,000, it picks up from there to

7,000 and then it charges hard to the 11,000rpm redline.'

Roland Brown of *Bike* magazine was to have a long association with the GSX-R over the coming years, buying and racing one as well as riding every single version. He wrote in June 1985: 'There's no flab or bullshit with the GSX-R750. This is the real thing. Only the committed (both senses) need apply.'

Roland Brown on the original GSX-R750. Roland would later buy and race his own machine, and as a respected freelance journalist he would test every model of the 750, 1100, and 600, as well as numerous specials. (*Bike* magazine)

The menacing twin headlight stare was pure Endurance racing. (Suzuki)

And the tail-end was tapered to a point. The grab handle was a pillion insurance policy. (Suzuki)

The handling of the machine was also universally praised, although the brochure's boast of a maximum 55° degree lean angle was never tested! Oxley wrote at Ryuyo: 'By going for fairly radical steering geometry Suzuki has managed to make the GSX-R steer as quick as a bike with a 16-inch front wheel. With a steering angle of 26 degrees and a very short wheelbase of 1,463mm (57.6 inches) the bike has the super-sensitive feel of a real racer. The GSX-R doesn't like to be pitched into a corner, it requires a more positive lean into the bend, but once in the bends the Suzuki is quite capable of making full use of its massive ground clearance.' One thing Oxley did comment on was a stability problem on the straight, which was dialled out with the addition of some extra pre-load front and rear. Here was a machine that was built for going round corners, not the straights!

Oxley would also take the GSX-R750 to the Isle of Man TT course in June 1985 – not to race, but to see how this thoroughbred racer with lights would handle the toughest and most demanding roads in the world. 'The GSX-R is not an easy bike to ride fast from the word go,' he reported. 'You have to know what you are doing to get the best from it – both from riding it and setting it up. The machine's forks are the

most sensitive I've found on a roadster. You can tell precisely what's going on beneath you and that's vital on a machine that dares you to ride hard like the GSX-R. The ground clearance is simply incredible – a pint to anyone who can deck the thing on the road solo (falling off doesn't count!). The bike's racetrack ancestry is emphasised by the fact that it took me longer to get the hang of the bike on the road. But work at it and the GSX-R will work brilliantly for you. Don't bother and the bike will feel ungainly and unhelpful.'

So what of the GSX-R's direct competitor that was launched the same year – the Yamaha FZ750? Certainly the FZ looked the better road bike, with a broader spread of power from its five-valves per cylinder motor (although many experts doubted the use of an extra valve in a multi-cylinder motor, claiming that four does the job; Audi and Yamaha and some single cylinder engine manufacturers nevertheless persist with this design).

In the real world the Suzuki had around 80bhp at the rider's disposal at its 140/70VR18 rear tyre, which was on average around 5bhp behind the class-leading Yamaha. But on the other hand the Suzuki weighed in at 25kg (55lb) less than the Yamaha and a startling 45.4kg (100lb) less than the Honda VF750F

Improving the breed: the 1986 and 1987 GSX-R750s

Resting on your laurels in the fast-paced world of motorcycle design is a sure way to lose the advantage and Suzuki didn't want to do that. So, to keep the GSX-R750 at the top of its game, the firm made some minor changes to keep it current for the 1986 and 1987 seasons.

For 1986 the GSX-R750G featured a longer swingarm which lengthened the wheelbase to 1,455mm (57.3in). The extension on the swingarm was between 20 and 25mm depending on what specs you believe. That endurance racing twin lamp set-up also benefited from brighter bulbs in the headlight – 65/50W up from the disappointing 45W items. In the cosmetic department the fairing had a taller bellypan, the exhaust heat shield was slotted and not perforated, and the seat was now a one-piece dual item. Some air ducts on the fairing were also revised and graphics were altered.

As the USA finally got their hands on the GSX-R750 in 1986, they also benefited from a limited edition model which was even closer to race-ready spec. The 'Double R' or GSX-R750R featured a number of changes, including: updated NEAS front suspension, radial tyres, amber halogen headlamps, single-seat, and a new aluminium-bodied rear shock with remote reservoir. A steering damper helped keep the wider bars from flapping, and this machine had fully-floating 310mm front brake discs. Engine-wise it had a lightened sprocket cover and a cable operated dry clutch. All in all it was 2.7kg (6lb) lighter than the standard machine but came in with a $2,000 premium. Most were to be sold to racers. This model never came to the UK, as Heron Suzuki – the UK importer – already had plenty of the standard machines and felt that to bring in a more expensive version would be a waste of time. The limited edition Double R did have some kickback for British and European riders the following year, though, as many of its features found their way on to 1987's GSX-R750H.

The GSX-R750H was fitted with the Double R's updated PDF forks, along with the steering damper and the braking system from the RR. The front wheel spindle was thicker (helping to act as a sort of fork brace to stop the front-end from flexing) and there was a redesigned front mudguard in white instead of black to go with the new colour and graphic schemes. Tyres and rims were wider and the bike had a gold coloured final drive chain. Finally, to accentuate the purposeful look, the fuel tank was redesigned, giving it a bulkier, hunched-forward look. Again, there was a limited edition model with a single-seat and a black and gold colour scheme.

Thankfully this was only the precursor to a completely new, second generation GSX-R750.

The 1986 GSX-R750G. (John Noble)

The Limited Edition was destined for the US market only, but parts did spin off to standard models. (Suzuki)

The H of 1987 featured wider rims and a host of improvements from the US Limited Edition machine. (Suzuki)

Interceptor, so what the Suzuki lacked in outright power it made up for in lack of weight.

After both machines were ridden by *MCN* – although not back-to-back – it certainly seemed as if it would be a real close call. Oxley had the difficult job of telling the paying public which would be the best buy: 'After our first impressions there is little to separate the Yamaha FZ750 and the Suzuki GSX-R750. Certainly on a racetrack the two would be closely matched, though the Suzuki's weight and less compromising design would possibly show in its favour. On the road the FZ's superior low-down power is an advantage, although again many bikers may prefer the Suzuki's raw edge.' Later in the year he added: 'The Yamaha FZ is a better all-round bike, anyone can climb on one and go fast. The Suzuki takes a little more skill and knowledge. But know what you're doing and you'll eventually go quicker on the GSX-R and because of that the GSX-R gives me more satisfaction than the FZ.'

In the USA, the old GSX700 had to soldier on for another year, while up north in Canada and across the pond bikers and racers were all enjoying the new GSX-R. When it did arrive in the States it was an instant hit. In February 1986 *Cycle* said: 'The GSX-R steers with remarkable lightness, handles even sand-strewn, bumpy corners with confidence-inspiring predictability and accuracy. Crisp carburation makes throttle transitions smooth and controllable. A feel of mechanical unity is at the core of the GSX-R and significantly, less

weight allows the bike to perform engine-wise at the same level as the more powerful Yamaha FZ750. This Suzuki convinces us that the future is low mass. The puzzling thing about the GSX-R is the race bike format. The GSX-R's riding position demands total commitment from the rider and maybe that's why Suzuki labels the GSX-R750 a race bike for the streets.'

American monthly magazine *Cycle World* prophesied correctly when, under the headline 'Changing the Rules', Steve Anderson prophetically wrote the following words: 'Sportsbikes will soon be divided into two categories: before the GSX-R and after.' He added: 'There's a revolution under way and you've likely never even heard of its architect. His name is Etsuo Yokouchi and his blueprint for change is the Suzuki GSX-R750.'

Overall, then, the Suzuki GSX-R750 was an enormous success, and deservedly so, but no one would have guessed just what heights it would go to, let alone its remarkable longevity. With the benefit of hindsight and more modern machines, many now criticise the GSX-R as a bit of a dinosaur, but it sparked the opposition off into a brace of copy-cat machines and would be the first in the long line of race replicas which we still live with and ride today.

But for the Suzuki GSX-R750 1985 was just the start of the story, as this machine would become a phenomenal success and spawn a whole host of versions, capacities, and related family members while the opposition did their best to catch up.

A brief history of Suzuki

More than 90 years ago Michio Suzuki founded his company in the small seaside town of Hamamatsu, Japan. His sole purpose in doing so was that he wanted to create better, more user-friendly weaving looms, and for the first 30 or so years of the company's existence that was its sole aim. Suzuki looms rapidly became more innovative and higher in quality than their competition, either at home or abroad. Soon they were actually displacing the machines of world market leaders Great Britain and the Netherlands.

Despite this success, Suzuki realised that he had to diversify into other products. He decided that building a small car would be the most practical new venture for his company. Building upon existing Suzuki technology, the project was started in 1937, and by 1939 several compact motor cars had been built. These were extremely innovative, as well as being an almost spooky foretaste of the future, as they featured a liquid-cooled, four-stroke, four cylinder engine. From just 800cc (50cu in) this engine could generate an impressive 13hp.

War intervened and the small cars were abandoned as non-essential to the Imperial war effort, Suzuki making farm machinery, heaters, and tools instead. Following the end of the war the company went back to loom making. In 1946 loom production increased after the US approved the shipping of cotton to Japan, but just five years later the cotton industry collapsed and Suzuki was faced with a colossal challenge – how to survive.

Michio Suzuki once again looked at the needs of the Japanese people, and he saw that what they needed was inexpensive transport. He therefore concentrated his efforts on building a motorised bicycle, which was to become the first ever Suzuki two-wheeler. His first effort was called the Power Free, which used a 36cc two-stroke engine. What made this unique was the fact that the rider could pedal without or with engine assist, or could disconnect the pedals and run with the engine alone, thanks to a double-sprocketed gear system.

The Power Free soon got a two-speed transmission and was joined by a more powerful 60cc version called the Diamond Free. By 1954 Suzuki was producing 6,000 motorcycles per month and had changed its name to Suzuki Motor Co Ltd. The rest proved to be history.

Time-warping to the late 1970s, we find Suzuki finally getting back into the car building business as well as making itself a reputation with a popular line-up of two-stroke bikes. Two-strokes were simple to produce, fast, and exciting. They were also smelly, noisy, and not particularly fuel efficient or eco-friendly. Times, it seemed, were a-changing. Honda had shown everyone the way to go with the world's first Superbike – the CB750 – a decade earlier, and had then been usurped by Kawasaki's equally legendary Z1. Now it was time for Suzuki to have a go at building a big capacity four-stroke, and the resulting GS series of machines proved beyond doubt that Suzuki was now a major player in the world motorcycle market.

The mid-1980s were a turning point for the company. It absolutely blitzed the motorcycle world at the 1984 Cologne show by revealing two 'hot' new models. One was the square-four RG500 two-stroke machine, clearly modelled on its historic two-stroke racing heritage, and the other was the GSX-R750. Since then the Suzuki motorcycle range has gained a greater and greater following and the GSX-R range has grown with it, spawning 1,100, 400, 250, 600, and 1,000cc versions, all bearing that now legendary moniker.

Developing power –

Slingshots, short-strokes, long-strokes, and water cooling

Suzuki and the GSX-R750 had given motorcycling a new über-class – the 750cc superbike category. This class was to sell to the public machines similar to those which would be raced in the new World Superbike championship, which would begin in 1988, as well as providing a continuing basis for the bikes which would take part in the World Endurance series.

As well as providing this homologation base for the race machines, the GSX-R750 was selling in spades. It was only a matter of time, therefore, before other manufacturers would attempt the same two tasks with one machine. Suzuki and Kawasaki went the mass production route. Both the GSX-R and Kawasaki's 1989 ZXR750 were to flood the dealers' showroom floors. Their specs differed considerably from those of the machines out on the racetracks, but they sold in big numbers and had big followings. Yamaha and Honda did it a little differently. The Yamaha FZR OW-01 of 1989 and the Honda RC30 of 1988 were closer to the racing ideal in terms of equipment, but they were at least double the price of the

opposition. Honda's RC30 would arrive in time to win the first two World Superbike titles in the hands of Californian Fred Merkel, while the Yamaha would arrive a year later, with the steel-framed FZ750 winning in 1988 with Fabrizio Pirovano on board and a certain Mick Doohan winning a handful of races that year on the more exotic FZR750R. Both manufacturers would hedge their bets by continuing to supply their FZ750 and venerable VFR750 road models, while as standard, both the inline four-cylinder OW and the V4 RC30 were more like racers with lights on. Clearly, with these new threats both on the road and on the track something had to be done to bring the GSX-R750 up to date.

Suzuki therefore began to work on the first major update of the GSX-R. Again, they drew largely on their experience in World Endurance racing – Suzuki had won the 1987 world title – to come up with a worthy successor. The 1988 GSX-R750J featured major changes to take on the opposition. The engine was updated by looking at five main points:
  • increasing charging efficiency in the combustion chamber;

The second generation GSX-R750, known universally as the Slingshot, featured a complete rework of engine and chassis. (Suzuki)

- decreasing mechanical losses in the engine;
- increasing valve rev limits;
- increasing cooling efficiency;
- increasing engine response.

To do these things the following changes were made. An updated TSCC (Twin Swirl Combustion Chamber) was used, which, along with a 2.5mm increase for the intake valves, 1mm on the exhaust valves, and longer valve duration, allowed more air into the chamber to help provide a more complete combustion for better efficiency and power. Suzuki engineers felt that a

shorter stroke would help lower mechanical losses in the engine, so the bore and stroke changed from the previous 70 x 48.7mm to a shorter stroke of 73 x 44.7mm. It certainly made the 750J a revvy little beast, which hit its max claimed power of 112bhp at 11,000rpm. To get there safely, the valves and associated valve gear featured lighter rocker arms and larger diameter valve springs to increase the valve rev limits. It worked. The 750J's motor was strong enough to buzz away to its 13,000rpm redline, which was GSX-R400 territory and even higher than Kevin Schwantz's 1987 Yoshimura race bike!

Increasing cooling efficiency was the next aim. Updates to the SACS cooling system with bigger diameter hoses and a 15-row oil cooler gave a 20 per cent increase in oil flow around the motor, increasing cooling efficiency by 48 per cent. Added to this was the inclusion of a pair of intakes in the front fairing on either side of the twin headlights. This was the Suzuki Condensed Air Intake (SCAI for short), which fed cold air through the fairing into the carburettor intake ducts to improve the efficiency of the carbs themselves. During the GSX-R750's early years Suzuki's various works and privateer racing teams had found that getting cool air to the carbs was essential to get competitive power from the oil/air-cooled motor during a long, hot race. Race paddocks around the world would reveal many ingenious and some not so ingenious methods of using pipes from old Hoover vacuum cleaners and asbestos to route cold air into the airbox. SCAI and its associated fairing holes were obviously the Suzuki works option.

Increasing engine response came with the help of a new bank of carbs for the GSX-R750J. These were called 'Slingshot' carburettors, and that name would become almost a byword for this particular model of GSX-R. These 36mm carbs were much lighter and thinner than the previous model's, incorporating an 'indexing ridge' through which fuel could flow more smoothly. Lighter slides in the carbs also meant softer return springs could be used, improving the response of the engine to movements in the throttle twist-grip. All this breathed through a new four-into-two satin black exhaust.

The original alloy frame of the first GSX-R750 had found itself being left behind by the sort of demands made on it by the chassis. Racers complained that the frame itself was flexing and many went to amazing lengths to stiffen it, even replicating another set of frame rails along the lines of the originals and welding them on. With

The short-stroke Slingshot in action. (Suzuki)

this criticism in mind, the 750J chassis engineers built a whole new frame. This followed the classic double-cradle lines of its predecessor and was again made from aluminium alloy, but this time it used much beefier 45mm box tube. Gleaning information from the 1987 Suzuka Eight-Hour bike, the chassis engineers married the tubes to 80mm alloy castings at the head stock and swingarm pivot point. This made the entire frame much more compact and rigid than before, Suzuki actually claiming a 60 to 70 per cent improvement in rigidity. However, it was also more complicated and heavier than the frame it replaced, featuring 38 parts rather than 26 and weighing in at 15kg (33lb), a full 7kg (15lb) more than its predecessor.

The frame was attached to a stiffer swingarm of new design along with an updated version of Suzuki's Full Floater suspension system with a Showa rear shock. Up front were 43mm Showa forks (bigger than last year's, but lighter) with adjustable preload and a 12 position rebound and compression damping adjustment. These were of a new cartridge-type design, using less oil than previous forks, which the Japanese reckoned made them feel more sensitive. Wheels were now 17-inch three-spokers,

replacing the 18-inch six-spokers of the older bike and, hopefully, their propensity to flex. This size of wheel was again seen first on the earlier GSX-R race machines, and featured hollow spokes and a front 3.5-inch rim and a rear 4.5-inch rim. Brakes were also almost lifted straight off the previous year's F1 racer. The 750J had two 310mm floating discs and race-developed Nissin four piston calipers. So exotic were these brakes that the previous year they were only available in limited numbers.

Overall, the new machine weighed in at 195kg (429lb), which was up from the original machine's 176kg (387lb). Five kilos (11lb) of this came from the motor, while a further 6.8kg (15lb) came from the frame. The 'more efficient' exhaust system added a further 3kg (7lb), with the excess being made up from other parts. In comparison, the Honda RC30 weighed in at just 179kg (394lb). One thing the J did have over its lighter brother was size. It was much more compact, being 83.82mm (3.3in) lower than the older model from the ground to the top of the fairing. More importantly it benefited from a shorter wheelbase – 1,410mm (55.5in) compared to the earlier model's 1,455mm (57.3in). Steering geometry was 24.83° of rake and 99mm (3.9in) of trail.

To tackle the likes of the OW-01 and RC30 on the track, Suzuki developed a race kit with the help of Yoshimura. The GSX-R750J hop-up kit featured a skimmed gas-flowed cylinder head to give a 13:1 compression ratio, along with forged pistons and polished valves. Different camshafts and narrower higher-rate valve springs, along with a beefed-up camchain and auxiliary oil cooler, helped the motor cope with the higher revs and increased power. Yoshimura's own 'Duplex' exhaust system was used to boost mid-range power, while a re-jetting kit for the Slingshot carbs was included along with a dry clutch kit, different drive sprockets, gearing, and a ride-height adjuster. It certainly sounds modest compared to race kits found on more modern machines, but the benefit was improved handling and another 10bhp.

When it came to the design of the new clothes for the GSX-R750J, the idea was to once again ape Suzuki's race machines. Rumour has it that during the design process the head of chassis development had pictures of the various World Endurance and TT F1 racers stuck into his project diary for inspiration. To prove this, the 21-litre flat-topped fuel tank even had an indentation in it where a race-style rapid-fill system could be placed. The overall design was smoother and certainly looked more aerodynamically efficient than the slightly slabby original. Suzuki engineers said the bodywork had the benefit of giving the 750J 11 per cent less drag than the previous model and 5.7 per cent less frontal area to the oncoming 160mph (258kph) plus wind. The bottom of the fairing joined together behind the front wheel in a V-shape, for increased ground clearance, while the tail unit also received more curvy lines and the rear tyre got an aerodynamic rear hugger which was bolted on to the swingarm.

Motor Cycle News was again the first to get a go on the new machine. Just like the first GSX-R750, the launch took place at Suzuki's Ryuyo test circuit near its Hamamatsu factory – a circuit that the GSX-R had gone around so many times that it could probably do it without a rider on board. Chris Dabbs came away very impressed with the Slingshot GSX-R. 'The old bike was really peaky,' he wrote in a November 1987 issue of *MCN*, 'but the new bike pulls cleanly with almost as much torque as an 1100 from as little as 3,000rpm all the way to the rev limit. There isn't a glitch in the power delivery and the carburation is super-smooth. Steering is better than the old bike, too, with less effort needed at the bars.'

Roland Brown from *Bike* magazine – who'd bought and raced one of the very first

GSX-R750s in the country in 1985, said of the J in April 1988: 'I can't remember the last bike that made me so keen to go out and ride it. On the racetrack against the new Honda RC30 it may or may not be competitive. On the road it can only be a winner.'

Grant Leonard from *Superbike* magazine agreed: 'The GSX-R750J has lost the previous version's tight, buzzy feel and revs as freely as the Kawasaki GPX750 – but up to 13,000rpmn. The real power lies between 7,000 and 12,000 but there's stacks low-down for hauling around, too. As a racer it has no peers in the sub-five thousand pound bracket, on the road and for everyday use it's not the most practical but is definitely the most fun.' The French – who were taking the 750 and 1100 to their hearts as well as winning endurance titles on the 750 – also reckoned it was the business, with the 750J winning *Moto-Journal*'s machine of the year for the second year in succession.

While many thought the 750J was a better road bike, there were two things that really held it back on the track. The first was the fact that the 750J's ground clearance was reduced from the original bike's by a quarter of an inch. February 1988's issue of *Cycle* reported: 'The new bike does everything more quickly and easier than the old. Stop, go, turn and drag the ground. The bike really forces a compromise between optimum suspension settings and ground clearance.' *Cycle World* agreed: 'When pushed aggressively the kickstand hits the ground on the left, the fairing drags both sides – even if the rider hangs off – and worse the 4 into 2 exhaust hits the pavement both sides.' The British magazines also noted the problem. *Superbike* said: 'It seems as if serious efforts have been made to lower the whole bike – particularly the front end. Suzuki may have gone too far here for trying to give it the look of a pukka race bike as for the race boys it has created a serious ground clearance problem.'

To counter this you either had to buy a higher-upswept exhaust system, replace the stock Showa shock with a race item, or fit a ride-height adjuster.

The second problem was that of tunability. With the original long-stroke motor, although mid-range grunt was a little lacking it was easier to tune the motor for the much-needed top-end power which was needed to win races. The short-stroke and more oversquare dimensions of the 750J gave it a more top-heavy powerband and tuners were finding it hard to get the sort of power they were getting from the older, long-stroke motors. Suzuki wouldn't be able to address this problem until the limited edition sports-production RRK of 1989 and the road-biased 750L of 1990. To make matters worse, some tuners and racers were finding that the combustion chambers were prone to cracking, with little bits of aluminium around the valve seats breaking off. Not nice.

One thing Suzuki did do for the 1989 GSX-R750K was address the ground clearance problems. Suzuki chassis engineers moved the rear shock's top mount 4mm lower and used fork tubes that were 6mm longer. Third, fourth, and fifth gear ratios were changed, with a lower second gear ratio. The exhausts now had shiny stainless covers to them, the brake lever was four-way adjustable, and wheelbase was up by 5mm. Overall looks were the same, although you now had a natty little single-seat cowling over the pillion as standard.

The improvements helped, but a new kid was on the block – the Kawasaki ZXR750H1. It was billed as the RC30 for the masses and was a pretty good first shot, although the GSX-R750K was a little cheaper, lighter, and had a slightly more usable engine. Kawasaki's ZXR would soon develop into a much more effective challenger of Suzuki's domination in the 750cc race-replica market.

The long-stroke returns

With the 1989 RRK sports production version reverting back to the long-stroke layout it was only a matter of time before the road-biased GSX-Rs did the same. So, for the 1990 model year the next version – the L – received the same long-stroke motor as the homologation racer, 70 x 48.7mm, altered valve angles, increased port velocity, and a host of other refinements. Chief among these was bigger Slingshot carbs, up to 38mm (although California-only models kept the earlier 36mm items for emissions), which had a non-functional power jet which eager tuners would soon liberate to free up a few more precious bhp. The new Mikuni carbs also now matched the reshaped inlet ports. The carbs sprayed fuel into the venturis at full throttle to compensate for a leaner main jet. Deeper inside, the connecting rods and associated bolts featured a lighter and stronger construction, with the rod bolts threaded into the rods themselves rather than using the traditional external, and heavier, nut-and-bolt set-up.

The L's pistons were smaller and lighter even than those on the 1985–7 GSX-Rs and now came with an Alumite covering, which Suzuki claimed improved surface hardness. The combustion chamber itself was domed, and to prevent the earlier problem of cracking between valves the spark plugs shrank to 10mm to give that area much more 'meat' around the valves. This was important, as the 750L had larger diameter intake valves (27mm, up by 1 mm, with 24mm for the exhaust valves), so the bigger 12mm plugs had to go. The cooling system itself was updated again. A curved oil cooler donated from the bigger GSX-R1100 allowed more surface area for better cooling, but in the same given frontal area. A new exhaust pipe was based on the RR's, now being four-into-two-into-one and stainless. To

improve ground clearance still further, the end-can itself featured a flat side near the join with the pipes for a precious few extra mm when right on the limit. Many of these internals came from the previous year's limited edition RR, which must have made people who forked out for the earlier machine a little bit sick. Piston speed was still up in the heavens, as despite the shorter stroke the L still redlined at 13,000rpm. The result was a claimed 114bhp (85kW), which equated to around 106bhp (79kW) at the rear wheel and in the real world. Getting that redundant power jet working again in those Slingshot carbs saw an increase to around 119bhp (88.7kW). Instead of the peaky delivery of earlier GSX-Rs, the L had a much more linear curve up to its peak output.

The chassis also underwent changes. The frame was largely the same, although the width between the two main frame rails was increased a little and rake was reduced to 25.3° with the trail remaining as before. There was also a 10mm longer swingarm, with thicker alloy walls which helped push the overall wheelbase up to 1,415mm (55.18in).

Suspension-wise, the 1990 GSX-R750 featured 41mm inverted or 'upside-down' front forks. In the crucible of racing, first in off-road and later on Tarmac, it was found that upside-down forks offered a degree of stiffness over conventional forks. GSX-R legend has it that Swedish rider Anders Andersson – who raced GSX-Rs during 1986 and 1987 in the TTF1 class – made his first inverted forks by cutting down a set of long-travel motocross forks. Unsurprisingly this talented racer and engineer was snapped up to work for Swedish suspension experts Öhlins. As Ducati's suspension technician, he later helped Carl Fogarty to two of his four World Superbike titles. Today, only the more austere supersport 600

It still had a purposeful profile. The Slingshot 750L awaiting action. (Bike)

machines and the likes of the Kawasaki ZX-9R Ninja have conventional forks. So, at the time they were the latest thing – although the USA's machines again were a little behind the times, carrying on as they did with conventional 43mm cartridge Showa items.

At the rear you had a remote reservoir for the rear shock, the main body of which was now made from aluminium rather than steel and also added compression adjustment to its repertoire. The reservoir hanging from the tail unit was almost to be a trademark look for the later oil-cooled GSX-Rs, but it also served an important

purpose. Distancing the reservoir from the main unit meant that it was less prone to heat up and go soggy – a criticism of the earlier model. The rear wheel also got a wider rim, up another inch to 5.5, now carrying a 170 rear-section Michelin radial as standard, but, with a nod towards racing, this meant that slicks could be fitted to the standard wheel. Brakes were also further refined. The earlier drilled discs were replaced with 5mm thicker slotted discs, which helped dissipate heat quicker. Calipers were Nissin four pots. Overall the earlier trend for the GSX-R getting heavier was reversed – but only just. The

The L saw a return to the long-stroke configuration after complaints that it was difficult to get good power from the reviver short-stroker. (Jason Critchell)

GSX-R750L weighed in at 193kg (425lb), just 2kg (4.4lb) lighter than before.

Despite these improvements, the L was going to have its work cut out to defend its position in the market. While exotica like the RC30 and OW-01 were racetrack flights of fancy for most bikers' wallets, the ZXR750 was – like the GSX-R – a race bike for the masses. In June 1990 *Motorcyclist* magazine in the USA pitted the new GSX-R against the RC30 and the ZXR (called the ZX-7 over that side of the Atlantic). The Yamaha FZR750R OW-01 rarely found itself on a road test as it was not US-legal. The testers found that the Suzuki topped the Kawasaki in a number of areas such as peak power and smoothness of response to the throttle. The 750L also impressed with its handling with standard settings. It was surprising, then, that the Kawasaki took the overall honours, with perhaps its substantial extra weight (233kg, or 512lb) making it a more viable proposition on the street. According to the boys at *Motorcyclist*, the extra money paid for the VFR750R was just not worth the small advantages it conferred on the road. Of course, the track proved to be a different ball game. Whatever the results, Americans found the 750L to be most impressive. It would break into the ten second bracket at the drag strip (clutch allowing), top 150mph (241kph) on a long enough road (highway patrol allowing), and pretty much give you more bang for your buck.

In the UK, though, the 750L was greeted with perhaps even more enthusiasm. It's strange now to look back a whole decade to find that even then the GSX-R was looked upon as an established family of machines, being around as it had for six years. Each new version was eagerly awaited and the L was no exception. In the June 1990 issue of *Bike*, Tim Thompson waxed lyrically: 'If performance is your game, these modern bikes are the dog's bollocks. And the GSX-R750L is back among the bestest – but still doing its own thing.'

Any sort of competition, be it war or racing, generally speeds up the development of machines. With the World Superbike series firmly established (if a little shaky from time to time) the protagonists involved also improved. Ducati were getting into gear with their 851 and 888 twins, although it would be another few years before they could get these achingly gorgeous machines into large-scale production for the masses. Meanwhile Honda and Yamaha carried on with their limited-run racers. However, Kawasaki were going to take the fight to the showroom floor for 1991 with a new version of the ZXR750.

The ZXR750 J1 was gorgeous to look at, with the trick-looking Hoover pipes going into the tank, stunning single colour paint jobs, and sharper, less angular styling than the earlier H1 and H2. It was just a shame that the rear suspension set-up was designed by the same person who came up with the idea for thumbscrews – it could be that painful, but in a more personal place. Added to this woe, the threat on the horizon of a 100bhp World Superbike limit meant that Kawasaki restricted the J1 to this figure.

Suzuki still felt it necessary to make some updates to the GSX-R750 for 1991. Internally, the 750M featured a single rocker arm per valve as opposed to one for two valves. So now individual cam lobes worked single, smaller

Superbike's John Cantlie lifts it up on a 750M. (Phil Masters)

rocker arms, which offered a reduction in inertia at high rpm of five per cent according to Suzuki engineers. The older forked rockers were just too big, heavy, and flexible at the sorts of rpm that the Suzuki revved to. Valve lash went from being adjusted by heavy threaded screws on the rocker arms to much simpler and smaller shims. The stiffer valve springs from the GSX-R1100 were used, while Suzuki engineers also revised the porting for the motor, altered the cam timing slightly, and reshaped the combustion chamber.

All these changes provided no extra power, according to Suzuki's claimed figures (114bhp again), but did mean that peak power could be held for much longer and probably gave tuners a better base to work from. The chassis remained the same – save for the US machines finally getting the smaller diameter inverted forks – and the inclusion of a steering damper as standard.

The biggest change was the bodywork. The stunning looks of the World Endurance

The L and M side-by-side highlight their aerodynamic differences. (Jason Critchell)

machines with their droop-snooted bodywork and faired-in headlights was a styling hit, as well as an aerodynamic necessity. These looks were replicated with the 750M, with the twin headlights recessed behind a clear plastic lens. The whole fairing itself was slinkier, featuring a raked screen, smaller frontal area, and reduced drag. Suzuki

The M featured twin tail lights. (Suzuki)

claimed that the design was lifted directly from their endurance racing machines of the previous year. The tail unit was also wider, as were the seats. The rear light now featured twin rectangular tail lights. All these revisions – however small – added up to an increase in weight. Apart from the previous year's L, the GSX-R was steadily putting on the pounds, with the M hitting the scales at 208kg (457.6lb).

Despite the extra weight the cult of the GSX-R was such that its 'power to the people' ethos meant more performance for less cash. *Cycle* magazine reported: 'Compared to the race-spec ZX-7R, the least expensive machine in the test – the GSX-R – is also the most impressive. It remains the weapon of choice for the street, offering superior suspension performance and near parity in acceleration all in the most accessible package.' In the April 1991 issue of *Bike*, Tim Thompson again passed judgement on the latest GSX-R. 'It's built for high-speed excellence and couldn't care about the rest. In fact, it's so near perfection now, that it's probably the best 750 built so far.' High praise indeed from a man who has confessed an undying love of the GSX-R's then-nemesis, the ZXR750, having actually bought one – the only sure sign of a journalist's bent!

The 750M caught itself a pair of notable scalps during *Motor Cyclist*'s test of the GSX-R, CBR600, and FireBlade, by taking the honours in this battle of the different capacity sportsbikes. 'Not only does the Suzuki do most everything right, it may have won simply because it does very little wrong, never taking less than second place in any category. Winning isn't a matter of dominating in every category, so far that's not been possible. The Suzuki took top honours by striking the best balance and in this class warfare that's enough to earn it the title of The World's Best Sportsbike.'

Liquid cooling – at last

The writing was on the wall for the old oil/air-cooled motor as both on the racetrack and in the showrooms the limit of its useful life was being reached. Suzuki had introduced a liquid-cooled 400 for the domestic market in 1990 with the GSX-R400RRL, so it was only a matter of time before its bigger brother got the same. In 1992 the water-cooled GSX-R750 finally arrived – the GSX-R750WN. It will remembered that the reasons why Suzuki had gone with oil and air cooling back in 1985 were the complexity and

bulkiness of the water jacket around the engine, but time had moved on and had now caught up with Suzuki. Firstly, the older motor was finding itself losing power as it fought to keep cool at such high rev ranges, so lower temperatures meant more power for longer. Also, seven years of development in design and manufacture meant that there was no longer such a weight and complexity penalty with water cooling and its associated jackets, pipes, and radiators. In fact, the latest motor would be lighter, slimmer, and more compact than its predecessor.

The 750WN itself was pretty much a completely new motorcycle. Suzuki engineers still kept some of the good points of the older motor, such as one oil pump which would continue to move oil around the engine and spray it on to the undersides of the pistons. The water-cooling system featured a curved radiator and a small 210mm (8.3in) diameter electric fan. Even the oil filter had water cooling, which would then cool the oil before it went on its way. Overall, the cooling system had twice the cooling capacity of the previous M. The bore and stroke of 70 x 48.7mm was retained, although thanks to the more effective cooling system the compression could be raised from 10.9:1 to 11.8:1 to help liberate a little more power. Pistons were now lighter than before. The valve train in the cylinder head was altered again, this time losing the rocker arms altogether, with the valve buckets now working directly off the cam lobes. Valve sizes were 27mm for inlet and 24mm for exhaust. The valves now had single spring operation and a reduced stem diameter down from 5 to 4.5mm, all saving valuable weight. The valve-included angle (the angle between the inlet and exhaust valves) was down from 40 to 32°, making the head narrower. The compact combustion chamber and increased compression ratio helped to raise the combustion efficiency of the motor and therefore power. Externally, apart from being much more

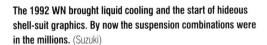

The 1992 WN brought liquid cooling and the start of hideous shell-suit graphics. By now the suspension combinations were in the millions. (Suzuki)

compact (width between the crankcases was down from 490mm to 433, thanks to a 40mm shorter crankshaft, and the width between the cylinders was reduced by 10mm) the motor still sported its old external fins, despite water cooling. Claimed power was 116bhp (86.5KW.)

Chassis-wise, rumours said that many engineers wanted to move to a twin-beam aluminium frame, similar to what the opposition were using, but certain key figures in the project, as well as the marketing men, felt that it wouldn't look like a GSX-R. The double-cradle was to stay, although it would undergo a thorough reworking. The frame itself was to be thicker and stronger than before, using computer design and featuring 60 x 45mm pentagonal cross-section mainspars, which improved rigidity by five per

cent and torsional resistance by 24 per cent. The subframe was now bolted, rather than welded on, which was a move towards quicker preparation for the track. The swingarm was all-new, featuring pressed aluminium sections which were laid out asymmetrically, so that the four-two-one exhaust had even more ground clearance. Wheelbase was up to 1,435mm (56in), but agility was improved with a rake of 24.5° (down 1° on the M) and a trail of just 94mm (3.7in). The rear shock had a different linkage, while the upside-down Showas first seen in 1990 were now updated with different spring and damping rates. The bike was also fitted with a non-adjustable steering damper. Braking was 310mm discs, but with the thickness back up to 5mm from 4.5mm and Nissin four-pot calipers. More refined and

Bike magazine's Phil West on the boil on the WN. He rated it as the best GSX-R yet. (*Bike* magazine)

snug-fitting bodywork helped give the new bike a lower frontal aspect, as well as a new tail light. Despite being narrower than the M the WN weighed the same – 208kg (457.6lb).

While scales and dynos around the world were confused as to whether the WN was a little heavier and perhaps a little less powerful than the Suzuki brochure claimed, many still saw the WN as an improvement – especially as usable power came in much earlier, at around 7,500rpm rather than the 9,000 of the older motor. Phil West in *Bike*'s August 1992 issue said: 'As an all-

The double-cradle GSX-R750 family from 1985 to 1994.
Superbike **tested the lot in 1994.** (Phil Masters)

round sportster-type chap of a 750 the GSX-R is pretty much unbeatable. Its motor is the quickest, most exhilarating if not as flexible as the all-rounder VFR. Its suspension is unquestionably the best in class and if its steering isn't quite the equal of the ZXR it more than makes up for it in other departments.'

In a back-to-back test against the very rivals mentioned, *Superbike* magazine backed up West's opinions by finding that the GSX-R was the clear winner in the performance stakes. It was 10mph (16kph) quicker in a straight line and half a second quicker down the quarter of a mile, and then in the twisties the Suzuki's superior suspension meant that the GSX-R could handle the bumps better. One grumble was that: 'This year's water-cooled variant has lost a little of the

traditional GSX-R rort. It feels smoother and less psychopathic than before.'

As usual, the poor old US of A had to wait a further year before they finally got their hands on the water-cooled machine, as Suzuki's American importers felt that the 750M was still selling well enough and was competitively priced. Instead of importing the machine everyone wanted, they simply stuck some hideous new graphics on the 750M. The irony was that the GSX-R600 which was on sale in the US at the time was actually a sleeved-down WN engine. Cleverly, *Cycle World* headed north into Canada to get hold of the new model, and found that their test machine could reach 158mph (254kph), making it the fastest production 750 they'd tested and only 1mph down on the GSX-R1100.

By now the competition in the 750 class was fierce. In 1994 the YZF750R was the performance yardstick. (Yamaha UK)

By 1993 Kawasaki had released the ZXR750L, which boasted further refinements, the most important being the switch from the emaciated 100bhp (74.6kW) motor to a full power 121bhp (90.3kW) version. Other changes included the removal of the Hoover pipes and the inclusion of a large ram-air duct on the left side of the twin headlights. More competition came that year in the form of the Yamaha YZF750. Yamaha's venerable OW-01 was past it in the racing stakes, to be replaced by the showroom floor YZF750R and the bog-standard racer the YZF750SP. It was going to be a hell of a fight. Despite the fact that the YZF wasn't available in the US, *Cycle World* managed to put the three 750s together for the first time on that continent. In a comparison between the three testers, it observed: 'The

Suzuki's dyno numbers are a disappointment. Liquid-cooling hasn't brought an increase in performance. Even with its power deficit the GSX-R wasn't that far off the pace and on the street the suspension was the most comfortable. The ZX-7 is quicker, faster, better on the racetrack than the GSX-R and easier to ride at speed.' On account of the YZF's unavailability in the US at the time, *Cycle World* excluded it from the results. It certainly looked as if the opposition was finally catching up with and passing the GSX-R.

Meanwhile, as the Americans were getting used to the WN in 1993, in Europe the GSX-R750WP was coming on-line, which was nothing more than a WN with changes to the graphics. It was 1994 before any major redesigning

1994 saw the GSX-R get a redesigned front fairing with multi-reflector headlamps. (Phil Masters)

occurred. The standard production model of 1994 was the GSX-R750WR, featuring 60 design changes, and it needed every one of them to take on the opposition. The motor had lightweight magnesium valve covers and side covers, hollow transmission shafts, a slightly redesigned exhaust system, and updated 38mm Slingshot carbs.

On the chassis side, weight had to be saved from some place, so the WR had thinner frame walls but with two cast aluminium head stays on each side of the engine to keep the rigidity up while taking weight down. The front forks were now 2mm bigger, being 43mm inverted items, but thinner stanchions meant they were still lighter – they were also a lovely shade of Alumite blue. The swingarm was now extruded alloy

rather than pressed, and featured a box-section endurance-style strengthener. The pivot shaft was beefed up from 20 to 22mm. Suspension rates front and rear were also altered, making it around 20 per cent stiffer. Brakes were the stunning six-pot Tokicos nabbed from the GSX-R1100 and the rear tyre grew in width to 180mm rear section. Clothing was subtly updated, with a more compact pair of multi-reflector headlights nestling behind a reshaped upper cowling and a slightly more relaxed riding position. It looked good and it was lighter at 200kg (440lb), although no more powerful, but by now the GSX-R was really starting to lose out to the opposition.

Superbike magazine's John Cantlie pitted the WR up against the ZXR750L2 (same as the L1), the YZF750R, and a Ducati 750SS in the March

The awesome front-end of the ZXR750L made it a superb handler. (Kawasaki UK)

Six-piston calipers debuted on the 1994 machine. (Suzuki)

1994 issue, and said: 'The GSX-R always had a reputation as the football hooligan of the 750s. Mad, bad and a bit dangerous to know, the Suzuki suddenly started to look a bit tame and flaccid as first the ZXR and then the YZF flashed past with greater horsepower and funkier styling. For me, the ZXR is the best supersports 750 of 1994.' Despite such a result, the GSX-R was allowed into *Superbike*'s 'New Sportsbike of the Year' competition in the October issue, as the ZXR was identical to the previous year's. Up against the new Ducati 916, the Honda RC45 (another V4 limited edition 750 for WSB racing), the Yamaha FZR600R, the Kawasaki ZX-9R, and Suzuki's RF900F, the GSX-R finished in third place behind the gorgeous V-twin Ducati and the hand-made exotic RC45. 'The GSX-R is in a

HAYNES GREAT BIKES SUZUKI GSX-R750

different world to the first two bikes in this competition, but it's a greatly improved bike. Motor needs thrashing and suspension needs tuning, but get it wound up and it flies!'

The final year of the old double-cradle framed GSX-R came in 1995, with the WS model. Changes were limited to graphics and the colour of the forks, but the overall design of the bike was long in the tooth and that conveyed distinct disadvantages. Firstly, there was only so much you could do with the engine position in that frame. It naturally 'sat-up' in between the rails,

which meant that it was hard to get the centre of gravity lower in the bike. This meant the bike – especially with a full tank of fuel – would feel a little top heavy and would drop into corners. Also, the position of the engine meant that downdraught carbs, which give the air a straight through route from the airbox into the carbs more efficiently, could not be used. But secretly, at Suzuki HQ in Hamamatsu, a new, more modern GSX-R was being developed, one which wouldn't be hamstrung by the fashions of the past but would set its own trends.

Sports production specials

With the hard-to-tune short-stroke 750L and 750K ruling the roads in 1988 and 1989, Suzuki realised that they needed a sports production machine for race homologation. Consequently in 1989 they released the GSX-R750RK. This 'Double R' model was limited to just 500 machines and featured the original long-stroke motor (70 x 48.7mm) but with reshaped intake ports, 10mm racing spark plugs, and 40mm Slingshot carbs. Deeper in the motor were lighter, stronger valves and

springs, beefed-up con-rods, and a magnesium valve cover. The oil cooler was larger and had a secondary cooler below it. The crankcase covers were also chamfered at an angle to improve ground clearance – an issue on the 750L. The RK had a six-speed close-ratio gearbox, a four-into-one stainless steel exhaust with a brushed aluminium end can, a 19-litre (4.2gal) alloy tank, and a wider 5.5-inch rear rim. The racing bodywork featured quick-release fasteners and a lower

The R was an homologation special to take on the likes of the RC30 and OW-01. Although today it's rarer than either, it was not as competitive as the Honda and Yamaha. (John Noble)

screen as well as larger diameter SCAI inlets. Overall, the weight of the RK was just 187kg (411.4lb). Power was boosted nearer to race levels by buying the Suzuki race kit, which included higher-compression forged pistons, cams, race exhaust, dry clutch, ignition box, different gears, and racing cam chain tensioners. Chassis parts included new forks, springs, rear shock, adjustable steering damper, ride-height adjuster, kill switch, and racing battery. Although on the track the RK lost out to the Honda RC30 and Yamaha OW-01, it now commands a rarity value that the other two machines don't have.

Steve Jones has a J-reg RK and he's your typical GSX-R fan, attending the August 2001 GSX-R day at Brands Hatch in Kent. 'I love it. My local pub in Wiltshire has regular bike meets and you get loads of guys turning up on Ducati 996s, but people always come over to look at my bike, I guess because there were only 500 made world-wide and just 50 in the UK. I've had a few GSX-Rs before this one, including an L, M, and a water-cooled WN, but I always lusted after an RK. I've had mine for years and it's an import and has a number of non-standard bits, such as a dry race clutch, and I replaced the white wheels with black ones to carry the bigger 180 rear section tyre, instead of the standard 160. The bigger tyre does rub against the torque arm a bit. I got to know Mick Grant quite well, who used to run the Suzuki race effort at the time these came out, and he let me into his

garage and just had boxes and boxes of stuff, which was handy as bits can get hard to find and they're pricey! The seat unit alone is a thousand quid and a full fairing is another £200!'

In the water-cooled years of the mid-1990s, Suzuki released another limited edition race machine, the 1994 GSX-R750SPR. Once more this race machine was to be aimed squarely at providing racers with a bike more suited to their needs. Only 200 of these would be produced – 150 for the German market and 50 for the French. The major alterations over the WR road machine were to the carbs, exhaust pipe, and gearbox. Wide-mouthed 40mm Mikuni flat-slide carbs replaced the 38mm CV items on the WR. The smoothbore carbs featured resin slides for improved throttle response. The ditching of the 38mm carbs was vitally important, as World Superbike rules necessitated the use of the same fuelling system as the homologation model. The SP had a much taller first gear as standard, with the other five closely-spaced for maximum acceleration. The motor breathed through an exhaust which had bigger header pipes than the standard ones, the SP's being 35mm – 3.2mm up on stock. Suspension was also more adjustable. Despite the 200 machines being sent to Germany and France, one Suzuki dealer – Paul Denning of Crescent Suzuki in the UK – got hold of one and raced it himself during 1994 and 1995. For Denning it was to be the start of his very successful Crescent Suzuki team.

Grant Leonard on the 1994 SPR. (*Superbike* magazine)

Racing successes

With the GSX-R being based on a race bike, it was obvious that the road bike itself would go back to its roots and end up on the track. 'Born on the race circuit, to return to the circuit' went the ad slogan. And so it was that in the UK in 1985 the *MCN* Superstock championship looked made for the new bike. It was a class for lightly modified road bikes, which therefore meant that costs could be kept to an absolute minimum. You could get yourself a machine ready to race for just four grand, and being so close to standard and in such a low state of tune, you had little to worry about on the reliability front. The regulations themselves would be a matter for conjecture, as jealous finger-pointing became rife when one rider or another took the advantage, but the frame was to remain stock, suspension modifications were unlimited, slick tyres were allowed, but engine mods were to be 'polishing and lightening only' along with a racing exhaust system.

Suzuki, Yamaha and Honda would enter teams, with the likes of Mick Grant and Trevor Nation on a GSX-R, Steve Parrish, Kenny Irons and Keith Huewen on the Yamaha FZ750, and Roger Marshall and Roger Burnett on the ageing VF750. To keep the 90bhp Honda competitive against the 100bhp Suzukis and Yamahas, Honda was allowed to make more changes to the motor of the VF, using different

cams, heads, valves, and pistons. Also, the front end of the obsolete RS860 – forks, brakes, and yokes – were grafted on to the front end.

Despite being in the twilight of a glorious career, Grant took the Heron Suzuki GSX-R to victory in the series, with an early dominant streak of four straight wins. Immediately the fingers began to be pointed, so much so that after his win at Donington Park the team offered the bike to be stripped by series technical referee Rod Scivyer. In *MCN* at the time Grant said: 'We just wanted to show people that there was nothing illegal about the bike.' The advantages that Grantie had, were probably down to the fact that his bike arrived early and the team had time to set it up to perfection, while the privateers had to wait until after the season started to get their bikes. Also, Grant had top mechanics like Paul Bolton and Nigel Everett (who would later work on the Harris factory Suzukis in World Superbike in 1996) to set the bikes up. The machine itself had open carbs, a Yoshimura pipe, a White Power shock, the front-end from the old 1,000cc Formula One bike (so much for cheap racing), and 16-inch wheels. In comparison, three-time winner Nation used a standard front-end and sometimes even the stock 18-inchers.

Grant – who had a right-hand gear shifter fitted to compliment his 'old-timer' style of non-

Mick Grant on the GSX-R he took to championship victory in
the *MCN* Superstocks. The front end was from a TTF1
machine. (Don Morley)

hang-off riding – was the man of the series by a
mile. 'We definitely had an advantage in the
early rounds,' he said, 'but it didn't take long
for the others to catch up and I had my work
cut out towards the end of the series.'

A series that used machines that were even
closer to stock was the ACU Metzeler Production
Championship. Here the machines were
standard, save for any modifications for safety
reasons. The GSX-R cleaned up, with Nation
(who swapped from Honda to Suzuki mid-
season) taking the title from Suzuki's Phil Mellor.

Mick Grant won titles with the GSX-R both as a rider and as manager of Team Grant, running the likes of Roger Burnett, Jamie Whitham, and Phil Mellor. (Mark Wernham)

Another mark of the machine's greatness was Grant winning the Production TT race with a stock GSX-R, while 11 similar machines finished in the top 15 places.

In the World and British TTF1 series it was a different matter. The peaky Yoshimura-kitted engines neither delivered the claimed horsepower, nor the reliability needed to take on the likes of Joey Dunlop and the sublime and torquey Honda RVF750. Despite losing out around 15bhp (11.2KW) to Dunlop's RVF, Grant still managed to come second to Dunlop in the world series, and second to Marshall in the British equivalent. One interesting story is that Trevor Nation even used to ride a GSX-R750, backed by sponsors Oxford Products, to the World TTF1 races. By the end of the year he had more than 3,000 miles on his own GSX-R, getting to and from events. However, there was some notable international success for the GSX-R. Canada got the machine the same year as Europe and Michel Mercier took the Canadian Superbike title with one. Future 250 and 500cc GP rider Juan Garriga also took two Spanish national titles on it.

In 1986 the GSX-R continued to impress on the

Schwantz and Whitham: two lions

track, and introduced two famous names to its history.

'Kevin Schwantz is 20 years old, lives in Houston, Texas; can be a real wise ass on occasion; and rides motorcycles. You may not have heard of him before but most likely you will. Because this kid Schwantz is the next great American road racer, and he's liable to end up world champion if the success and fame and glory and riches he's sure to earn along the way don't side-track him first.'

Respected racer, journalist, and talent spotter John Ulrich wrote that immediately after Schwantz had raced the Yoshimura Superbike in his try-out at Willow Springs on 2 December 1984. Thanks to Ulrich, Schwantz was signed to Yoshimura for the 1985 season to try and make the long-in-the-tooth GS700 competitive, while the rest of the world had the much better GSX-R750 to use. Yoshimura didn't plan to do the whole schedule of races that year, but Kevin's talents still shone through as he won three rounds and came second to Honda's Fred Merkel. With the skills of Schwantz on board, Yoshimura signed up for a full campaign in 1986. In Peter Clifford and Shirley Schwantz's book *Kevin Schwantz – The World's Champion*, Kevin recalled: 'It started off good, I was second at Daytona behind Eddie Lawson on the Yamaha. Wayne was fourth behind Merkel. But we had a lot of problems with the new GSX-R. I was leading Laguna by about five seconds ahead of Merkel with just a few laps to go and blew the thing up coming out of the last turn. It made a horrible noise right in front of the pits, right in front of all the Yosh guys and the main guys from

US Suzuki! I made a couple of mistakes and we had a bunch of trouble with the bike all season. We kept trying to get it to stay together, they'd slow it down every time trying to make it hang together and I guess I'd push it that much harder trying to keep up.' Eventually it would be Merkel and Schwantz's future GP nemesis Wayne Rainey who would battle for the championship that year, with Fred just nipping it after Rainey crashed out at Mid Ohio.

With the promise of Kevin's talent in 1985 and then the prospect of the new GSX-R750 in 1986, the sum didn't really add up considering the potential of the two parts. For Suzuki, one scrap of comfort on the North American continent came from Gary Goodfellow's Canadian 750cc Production title. One hint of what was to come in Schwantz's future came at the annual Trans-Atlantic match races on 16 March 1986. This meeting was special, as it was the UK's first good look at Schwantz. For the first time the races would be run at the newly extended Donington Park circuit, with the Melbourne Loop built to allow the circuit to reach the minimum length for Grand Prix regulations. The UK team featured legends such as 'Rocket' Ron Haslam, Rob McElnea, Keith Huewen, Steve Parrish, Roger Marshall, Roger Burnett, a young Kenny Irons, and Paul Iddon. Compared to this mass of UK talent, the US and Canadian teams were weak when measured against previous years, when they could boast the likes of Kenny Roberts, Freddie Spencer, Eddie Lawson, and Randy Mamola. Instead, John Ashmead, Dan Chivington, and Michel Mercier were included – names that were unknown on this side of the

Schwantz (number 34) on his GSX-R battling the likes of Nation (25) and Merkel (1) at the classic Trans-Atlantic race of 1986 at Donington Park. (Don Morley)

Atlantic. Two youngsters stood out in the American team: the gangly young Texan Kevin Schwantz and blonde, bronzed Californian Fred Merkel. It would be these two gregarious characters that would take the fight to the Brits.

Schwantz takes up the story in *Kevin Schwantz – The World's Champion*: 'I was down to ride Tony Rutter's bike, the bike he rode in the Isle of Man TT. The only problem was when I got there, everyone from the States had shipped their Superbikes over, Yoshimura at that time didn't want to send a bike. I got there and everyone was uncrating their immaculately prepared bikes from home. I said, "so where's my bike?" And

someone pointed over to this old sad looking yellow GSX-R sat in the corner with a shifter on the right hand side and a big puddle of oil underneath it. "You've got to be kidding," I said. I was lucky though because Keith Reed from Heron Suzuki worked on the bike and he sorted things out pretty good in a real short time. He had to manufacture a way of getting the shifter back over to the other side. Where it was leaking from was around the right hand shifter shaft seal because I think that a hole had been chiselled in the cases and an oil seal from a World War II fighter plane had been Araldited in place. The bike looked in general very very sad but it was

A study in concentration, 'Mez' Mellor (left) and Trevor Nation
line up at the start of a production race at Thruxton in 1986.
(Don Morley)

real real fast. It must have been as light as you could make a GSX-R back then. Our Yoshimura bike must have been 390 or 400lb (177 to 181 kilos). We used to have to put twenty or thirty pounds of lead on them for US Superbike races but this bike wasn't built to those regulations and I guess it was a 350, 360lb (159 to 163 kilo) bike. It ran well, and had a real good strong engine in it.'

The opening leg confirmed Schwantz's speed, but he crashed out while leading, after picking wets for a drying track. Against the British hordes, the only North American name in the top six was Merkel. The second race saw Schwantz and Merkel get past the Brits for a one–two. By the start of day two, the Brits were ahead 177–87. In a wet leg six, Haslam was out on the stock road-going VFR750 that the Honda importers had told him to ride. The legendary Barry Sheene, who was doing the commentary on the races, reckoned it was 'a bloody disgrace' that he should have such a stock machine. Despite this lack of power, Haslam reeled in race bike after race bike to come in fourth place, behind Merkel, Schwantz, and Burnett – who was riding the considerably more exotic RVF Honda. With points at 256–140 in favour of the Brits, they could not be caught; but then again, it was Schwantz who was heading for the £5,000 first prize for highest individual score. As the teams headed into the final race, the Texan led with 72 points, Burnett's consistency had put him in second with 65, with Merkel just a point behind.

The sun was out for the race, but the track was wet. Merkel opened up a healthy first lap lead ahead of Burnett and Schwantz. Yet again Haslam used the forgiving power characteristics of the road VFR to get into fourth position, before slipping past Burnett for third. Eventually Schwantz would keep second, behind leg winner Merkel, to take the prize. His performance on the 'sad looking yellow GSX-R' would give the world a wake-up call as to Kevin Schwantz's talents.

Merkel's too, as the Californian would go on to notch up two World Superbike titles in 1988 and 1989.

Another charismatic young rider got his first taste of GSX-R power in 1986 – Jamie Whitham. Whitham still remembers the first time he got to ride one. 'I'd never had or ridden road bikes up until then as all I had ever done was spend my money on my racing bikes. Up until 1986 I'd been riding 125s. I'd not done too bad and was starting to get reasonable results in European Championship races on it and was doing steady in the odd GP. Then Mick Grant rang me. I knew him at the time, as we lived near each other and to be honest he was a local hero. Well, he told me that despite being a real good class, I was wasting my time on a 125 and that I should "get myself on a big bike because that's all that people are interested in." He had a word with Suzuki and at the time Rex White was running the show with Mez (Phil Mellor) riding. Superstock were the big thing at the time. Granty had won it the previous year and pretty much in '86 you needed a GSX-R or an FZ to do any good. I tested the bike and people were happy, and I ended up racing it at the Powerbike meeting at Brands Hatch near the end of the season. Best result that weekend for me was seventh which was a good result, especially against the likes of Roger Burnett, Roger Marshall, Trevor Nation, Chris Martin, Paul Iddon, Mez and the like. The conditions played into my hands that weekend, really, as it was dry and wet and I chose the right tyres for the job. The amazing thing was that this was my first ever race on a four-stroke – I'd never ridden them before. I was shit scared of that bike, it was like a big horrible tank. Jumping from a little 125 on to that was a shock. My little 125 was a beautiful thing. It had so little power that to get the best out of it, it had to handle proper and it did that. Then I found myself on a big tank like the GSX-R. Now, I'm not being derogatory about the big

Suzuki, that's the way things were then, even though the GSX-R was lighter and handled better than most of the other things out there. Things were like that then, they were in a transition period. Today the GSX-R1000, Yamaha R1 and others have geometry settings and wheelbases that are like race bikes, but things were different then. It was just such a compromise when you set it up. I still say to this day that on big bikes, it's not the person who sets the bike up to perfection who will win, it's the person who can ride it when it's in a state. After the Powerbike meeting the Suzuki people were so happy as I'd beaten their main guys so that sowed the seeds for me for the next year as well.'

In 1986 the factory Suzuki team for the World TTF1 was the Skoal Bandit Suzuki team. This was a UK-based effort set up by Heron Suzuki. Rex White was at the helm with riders Paul Iddon and Chris Martin. For the World TTF1 championship, the early championship leader was Anders Andersson on a GSX-R backed by the Swedish importer. The opening round at Misano was a disaster for the team, but one Aussie far from home did shine – Rob Phillis. Phillis ('Syph' to his friends) made a one-off appearance and finished third. Later that year he would take the Australian title on his Yoshimura GSX-R. Andersson's lead was not to last, as the indomitable Joey Dunlop would take the title on the Honda at the penultimate round in Finland. At the Donington Park round, Martin had been injured and was replaced by former privateer Neil Robinson. 'Smutty' Robinson did well on the bike, winning the final round at Dundrod. Sadly, Robinson would die soon after at Scarborough's Oliver's Mount circuit. Iddon's Jerez win helped him to the runner-up spot behind Dunlop, with Andersson third and Robinson fourth. In the British series, Iddon would win at Silverstone and finish fifth overall behind winner 'Captain' Mark Phillips on his Suzuki RG500, despite not taking part in the full calendar of races.

In other classes, the Suzuki once more took the series win in the Metzeler Production Championship for 750cc machines with Phil Mellor on board, but Grant's Superstock win was not to be repeated for the GSX-R, as the Yamaha FZ750 of Kenny Irons took the top slot with five wins. The highest placed Suzuki was Keith Huewen in third.

In this year Suzuki began the first GSX-R Cup. Initially it began in the US, with big money prizes for the riders. One big name who came out of financially induced retirement to chase the big cash prizes was Doug Polen. The GSX-R cup would net the Texan $90,000 as he won 45 out of the 51 races that year. Eventually, other big names such as Jamie James, Scott Russell, and Aaron Yates would make their marks in the event. With the popularity of the Stateside event would come the Suzuki GSX-R World Cup. From 1988 until 1993, some of the best riders in the world would be invited by Suzuki to take part in the races, which would use identical, standard GSX-Rs straight out of the crate. To say that the racing was exciting was an understatement, and the later events even benefited from TV coverage.

In 1987, Schwantz and the Yoshimura Suzuki started to come good. Taking advantage of the AMA rules meant that the Yoshimura GSX-R was 768cc and was now pumping out around 138bhp (103KW) at 12,000 revs at the gearbox sprocket. This was a very special machine, using Showa suspension and Nissin brakes, and was rumoured to cost around $55,000.

Despite falling while leading at Daytona (where rival Rainey won), Kevin managed to claw his way back, coming to the last round at Sears Point with four wins. His eagerness for the start of the heat race meant he jumped the start, was given a minute penalty and was therefore posted as finishing last, which meant a position at the very back of the grid for the final. Rainey's mechanics wound him up, saying that he needn't bother racing, but that just made Kevin all the more determined. Within two laps Schwantz was dicing with Rainey, trying to force him into a mistake. It wasn't going to happen. Within five laps Kevin had the lead. It was all he could do to try and take the title, but Rainey did just enough to take the series win. Positive points were that Schwantz and the Yoshi Suzuki had showed that they were the main title threat, while the team and rider Scott Gray had taken the Formula USA title with a much-modified GSX-R750.

At the annual Trans-Atlantic Match races, the rivalry between Rainey and Schwantz spilled over once more, as the Brands Hatch and Donington Park crowds thrilled to the fairing-bashing antics of both riders, who were supposed to be on the same side. Schwantz ended up the winner by just three and a half points and so took the £5,000 prize.

Whitham was also continuing his association with the GSX-R. He recalled: 'In 1987 old Granty did a bit of a "Supermarket sweep" thing at Suzuki HQ and basically nabbed me a bike and some other bits and bobs for it. That year we did Superstocks and also had the odd go in the Super One series. That was pretty much an anything goes series for 750 to 1,300cc machines. Roger Marshall had a bike that he called "The Beast" which had an 1100 motor in it with loads of trick stuff, TTF1 frame and the like. We just used to slot the 1100 motor into our 750 frame to take part in the races. If we had time to do it, we'd swap the motors back so I could do Superstock, if not, I'd just do the Super One races. I remember getting the 1100 motor from a scrappers which had one of the new 1100s that had suffered a massive front-end smash. It was a write-off and the poor bugger had died. We slapped some flat-slide carbs on the motor and slipped it in. I had a few good results that year and towards the end of the year I was as steady as anyone

out there.'

In fact, Whitham won the last two rounds of the Superstock series that year, although it was never going to stop Huewen winning on the FZ Yamaha. Marshall would win the Super One and the similar Motoprix in dominant fashion on 'The Beast', while Mez Mellor would again take the Metzeler Production 750 title on the GSX-R.

In World TTF1 racing the championship would be taken by Italian Virginio Ferrari on the Bimota, by three points from Joey Dunlop. The Skoal Bandit Suzukis of Iddon and Roger Marshall were fast and reliable, but early season crashes meant that by the last round at Donington Park Iddon had at best an outside mathematical chance of the title. Iddon won (and sparked a furious team row with Marshall over the use of smaller, more fuel-efficient carbs, thus not having to stop for fuel during the race), but behind him seventh place gave Ferrari the title.

Short-stroke racing

Schwantz's meteoric rise to the top continued in 1988 with a factory Suzuki contract in 500cc GPs. Initially, he thought about plunging into a hectic trans-Atlantic schedule to take part in GPs and the AMA's Camel Pro Series, but decided instead to concentrate on Europe. His replacement in the Yoshimura squad was Doug Polen, who'd proved, perhaps more than anyone, the abilities of the GSX-R. Schwantz was to do one AMA ride, though, the Daytona 200. Yoshimura put together another very special machine for the Texan's assault on the legendary race. Officially, the short-stroke motor pumped out the same sort of power as the previous year's bike, but acceleration was

Schwantz on his way to second place at Daytona in 1986.
(Suzuki and Don Morley)

much improved. Hand-prepared Showas were front and rear along with factory Nissin calipers and discs.

When practice came Schwantz found the new bike was actually a little slower than the older ones being used by teammates Polen and Scott Gray, but still set pole position. 'I lose one second on the banking but can gain two on the infield.' He eventually converted pole into a race

Schwantz eventually won the Daytona 200 in 1988. Second was his teammate Doug Polen (number 23) on his 1987 machine. (Suzuki)

win of 90 seconds over teammate Polen, on Schwantz's 1987 machine. It was Suzuki's first 200 win ever on Daytona's famous 31° banking, and the first Suzuki win there since Wes Cooley on the GS1000 in 1981. 'Early on it was real close,' said Schwantz to reporters. 'I began to wonder if I would get away, but when I did things went real smooth. It's great to win here.' In the AMA season proper, Honda again took the title, with Bubba Shobert ahead of Polen. Schwantz and Rainey, meanwhile, shipped their private war over to Europe and GPs.

Suzuki decided to scale down its efforts on the world scene in 1988, ignoring both the TTF1 and the new World Superbike series. Despite this, one of the Japanese factory Suzukis in the hands of a Kiwi by the name of Gary Goodfellow earned Suzuki its first ever WSB win in race one at the Sugo racetrack in Japan. Private Suzukis which also appeared in the results for the fledgling new series were piloted either by canny locals (like Marshall's fourth in the first ever WSB race at Donington) or by Anders Andersson, who put up a fine show to get some excellent top

Jamie Whitham was linked for many years with the GSX-R. This is the TTF1 bike in 1988, the year he won the 750cc Production title on the short-stroke machine. (Don Morley)

ten placings.

Meanwhile, in the UK, the official Suzuki team was run by Mick Grant, who took over from Rex White, and the riders were Whitham and Mellor. Whit said: 'For 1988 we got the new 750J Slingshot with the short-stroke motor. It was nice and revvy and felt a bit lower and more like a race bike. Problems we had were to do with ground clearance and the fact that the suspension wasn't the best straight out of the box. I guess that's just because the Japs don't know if the bloke buying it is 15 stone and has an 18-stone wife who wants to go pillion on it, or if the guy's 10 stone wringing wet in his leathers. Well, two or three races in and people are ditching the 750 and either plumping for the 1100

(which at the time was still the old slab-sided one, but with 17-inch wheels) or use the Yamaha FZR1000. People like Trevor Nation and Ian Simpson were swapping over to other bikes, but we persevered with it – we had to! First track we had trouble on was Thruxton – bumpy and very fast. By the time we were at Snetterton, we managed to get a GSX-R1100J and used that for one round and one round only.'

The team's perseverance paid off, as Whitham won the series. 'What did help that year were the tyres,' he added. 'We were contracted to Michelin and to be fair we'd struggled a bit. Then at the third round at Carnaby, Michelin gave us some new tyres. They looked the same as the previous ones, but were completely different,

Polen would take the 1989 All-Japan TTF1 series, as well as the F3 with the GSX-R400. The previous year he gave Suzuki its second World Superbike win at Sugo. (Suzuki)

new construction and everything. That was the transformation. Soon as I rode on those tyres I knew that I could win it.'

Jamie was also second in the TTF1 series that year, behind Darren Dixon on a RG500 race bike: 'He'd had a good run early on when I struggled.' Add to that fifth in the 600 series on the GSX-F 'Teapot' (which paddock rumour said was bored out to nearer 750) and it was an impressive year. 'People who said it was a 750 are wrong. It was just brilliantly put together. Granty just uses the rulebook differently to anyone else. He looks at the rules and if they don't say he can't do something, he'll do it. Clever bloke is Granty. That year with Proddie racing, TTF1 and the 600s you'd be so busy with so many bikes, you'd find

Whit was back on a GSX-R in 1991 and doing well. (Don Morley)

yourself heading for a corner and would forget whether to go down two or three gears!'

At the TT the new Honda RVF750R RC30 was cleaning up, but Whitham still did well to get fourth in the Supersport 750 race. In the Superstock series, the RC30 won every round. Suzuki decided not to take part as the series was now run on a Dunlop control tyre.

For the 1989 season, the threat of the RC30 and the soon-to-arrive Yamaha FZR750R OW-01 meant that Suzuki had to give their race machine a shot in the arm. The GSX-R750RRK of 1989 helped, but was still woefully short on specifications compared to the Yam and Honda. Still, it did win the AMA series at last for Yoshimura with Jamie James on board (teammate Scott Russell was second). James also followed this up with a win in the Supersport 750 class. Polen – now racing in Japan – took the All-Japan F1 title with the GSX-R750 and the F3 title on the GSX-R400. He made it two wins for Suzuki in the World Superbike series as well, winning the wet first race at Sugo.

Whitham's year was up and down on the Durex-backed Suzuki. 'We decided to do Daytona and this was the first time V&M Racing got into the Tarmac stuff. Jack Valentine and Steve Mellor had pestered Granty for a motor and he relented. It was bloody fast! But then it dropped a valve. I think the valves they were using were ones they used in sprint and drag racing and the like. Thing with Daytona is that you're at full throttle for quite a while up there on the banking and while those valves may have been strong enough for sprints and the like, they weren't strong enough for Daytona. That year I fell off at the Ulster GP and broke my ankle. Two rivets popped out of the front brake disc and jammed it on. So that was that and I was out that year from about August onwards, which was a pain as I was doing well in all the championships. I was leading the Proddie series when I fell and still ended up third.' Sadly, the team also suffered the tragic loss of teammate

'Mez' Mellor, who died while on a GSX-R1100 in the Production TT.

The start of the 1990s heralded a return to the long-stroke road bike, although the short-stroke RRK was still around on the track. In the USA, Doug Chandler would take the title for Kawasaki, but Polen would return from Japan and a serious foot injury and make a one-off return to win impressively at Road Atlanta, while French Canadian Miguel DuHamel – son of 1970s ace Yvon – would win the penultimate race of the year.

In the UK, Durex backing continued for Team Grant, but without Whitham, who'd had a big offer from Honda Britain to partner Carl Fogarty. It was not a happy year for Suzuki or Whitham. Jamie struggled to get to grips with the front-end of the Honda, while his replacement at Suzuki, the experienced Roger Burnett, was finding it hard to hustle the Suzuki in the same way that Whitham or Mellor had.

With the final year of the oil/air-cooled GSX-R in 1991, Whitham returned to the fold. And Whit was more than happy to return. 'I'd just had a disastrous year on the Honda RC30 so in the end I was happy to go back to Mick and a competitive ride with Suzuki. To be honest I felt that I'd had such a shit year I almost didn't deserve to get much for 1991. Soon as I sat on that bike – which was pretty much the same old 1989 TTF1 bike – I felt comfortable. It was like getting back into an old comfy sofa. It was brilliant. Again that year I came third, I think, in the Supercup and won the TTF1 series, which ran alongside it.'

While the Suzuki wasn't the most powerful machine out on the track, Whitham could really make it work beneath him, with his unique ultra hang-off style. Whit's bike now featured two huge scoops in the screen, which routed cold air towards the carbs, as, researching into other GSX-R runners, Grant had found that too much heat was robbing the motors of power in long races. It was one of the many 'make-do-and-

After Whit's successful return to Suzuki in 1991 the new
liquid-cooled machine was a disappointment, Whit nicknaming
it 'the ironing board.' But he still impressed. Here he leads
Fogarty's Ducati and Rob McElnea's Yamaha. (Mark Wernham)

mend' things the critically underfunded team had
to do to survive and be competitive. 'Mick made
these scoops that jutted out into the airstream in
the screen. These fed cold air into the carbs. You
see it all the time on bikes nowadays, but that
was Mick. He is an innovator and very, very
clever. He and Butch [Cartright] used to make all
sorts of bits for that bike, even yokes and that.
Mick had an old universal mill, a lathe, and a TIG
welder. Good job they were good like that,
because there was hardly a meeting that went by
without that old frame cracking! The frame dated
from late 'eighties. It was probably the 1987
XR55, or something. Think about it. How many
race seasons do the Japanese expect to get out
of those frames? One, max, and yet there we
were riding this bike which by looking at it
everyone must have thought was a pile of shit –
but it wasn't! It was fast enough and it handled.
That year our team was superb. Mick and my
mechanic Butch Cartright did everything to make
that bike work.'

Over in the States 1991 was a lean year with
Yoshimura riders Mike Smith and Tommy Lynch,
who due to injuries and un-competitiveness
failed to score a win all year. In the Supersport
750 class, Russell won on the Kawasaki, with
Suzuki's Britt Turkington second.

The following year should have been a great
one for Suzuki. The problem that many tuners felt
hamstrung the potential power gains from the
GSX-R – oil and air cooling – was to be ditched in
favour of liquid cooling. Whitham decided to stick
around with Team Grant. 'Despite a great year in
1991, I still didn't have any other offers,' he
admitted, 'but I wanted to stay with Mick and
Butch anyway. Mick said at the end of 1991 that
a new bike was coming along. This would be the
business, water-cooled and dead fast. Of course,
when it came we still didn't have much of a
budget to change things and it wasn't as good
as the older bike.'

With the competition much tougher than

Revvin' Kevin

Kevin Schwantz is perhaps one of the most popular motorcycle racers ever. Always associated with number 34 – which was his uncle's race number – he rose quickly to be a contender for the AMA Superbike title, before moving to 500cc GPs with Suzuki. He still remembers when he first saw the GSX-R750. He said: 'After riding the GS700 in 1985, to see this thing … the GSX-R750, was amazing. It was like, "Holy shit, that thing looks like a race bike!"'

Three seasons in the AMA did not yield the title, but he certainly had fun. 'I really enjoyed those Superbike racing years. When I started racing it was just pure fun, when I got to riding the Superbike it was still a lot of fun plus it was neat that a lot of people wanted to talk to you, meet you and hear about the bike and the racing. Those years '85, '86 and especially '87 were probably the most fun that I have had racing.'

Throughout his career, in Superbike or GPs, Kevin made the most out of an amazing natural talent on machines which, perhaps, weren't the best out there.

But what is the difference between riding a Superbike and a GP bike? 'Even today you can still muscle a four-stroke around easier than a 500. What makes the 500 more trying to ride is that little bit extra. To ride a 500 well you really need finesse. You can make a superbike hard work, but hard work for a GP bike is something completely different. You need that finesse of throttle control when you are hard on it. You have to come up with a good way to convince the bike to do what you want it to do.'

His early win-or-crash attitude gave way to a more measured approach, which earned him the 1993 500cc World Championship, but fans around the world loved his post-win celebrations.

He still has a soft spot for his British fans. 'As the team was based in the UK, for me, I always felt like the Brit GP was my home GP. I had such shit times at Laguna Seca on the 500, and anyway, California is like a different country to Texas anyway. I always seemed to do really well in the UK and I appreciated the fans there, too.'

After he retired from bike racing in 1995 he took to

The style that took the 1993 500cc championship first came to the world's attention on a GSX-R750. Here's Kevin in action in 1986 at Daytona. (Don Morley)

racing cars and trucks and still keeps his links with Suzuki. 'I now run a Suzuki race school in Road Atlanta which I started in May 2001, and have my own clothing range, Brand 34. Suzuki spent a lot of money on the track to make it real good and I live about 200 miles from the track, which is cool. It's fun teaching people how to ride. It's great seeing all the pupils with different levels of ability at the school, with all of them wanting to improve. We have guys turn up who race and want to improve, and even people who have never been on a track before, but who want to experience riding around a track and want to improve machine control.'

Schwantz continues his association with the GSX-R to this very day. Here he is enjoying his time at the GSX-R Festival at Brands Hatch in August 2001. Behind him is rally star Colin McRae. (Suzuki)

before, Whitham was finding it hard going. 'At that time there were a lot of good bikes on the grid. The Nortons were bloody fast, there were a lot of good RC30s and OW-01s out there, and the Kawasakis were the bikes to beat in the hands of Brian Morrison and John Reynolds.' Many times Whitham would cross the line in the top five, normally behind the Nortons and the Kawasakis, and look to the pit-wall and just shrug as if to say 'what else can I do?'

Whitham could win on a bike without a power advantage – he'd shown that the previous year – but the new machine was harder to set up for his loose style, despite a custom-made JMC swingarm, Ohlins rear shock, and Showa forks and triple clamps. He added: 'It was like going back to the old tank GSX-Rs. We called it the ironing board, it was that flat and long. What could we do? We simply didn't have the money to make it go really well. I really couldn't ride it any harder than I was, to be honest.' Jamie eventually ended up in sixth position overall and scored 11th and 14th places at the Donington World Superbike round. The sad state of Suzuki's racing affairs was also reflected in the US, where they soldiered on with the older oil/air-cooled machine. The Yoshimura bikes struggled to make the top ten.

Quick Whit

If ever there was a British Schwantz, Jamie Whitham is it. Like Kevin, he has his own unique riding style (he sticks his neck out, figuratively and literally) and is one of the most popular British riders around. After racing 'little' bikes, Jamie moved to racing production-based machines towards the end of 1986. As well as his successful early GSX-R years, he was double British champion in 1993 on the Fast Orange-backed Yamaha YZF, and won a World Superbike race the following year on a factory Ducati 916 along with two other podium positions, before returning to the UK to try to reclaim his British title. That year, 1995, he won 11 races out of 16 but still had to concede the title to rival Steve Hislop – the reason was that he'd been diagnosed with Hodgkin's disease, lymphatic cancer. His fightback was unsurprising, if you knew him. 'It puts everything into perspective,' he said. 'I'm looking forward to going to hospital for something normal like a broken leg.' After successful chemotherapy, his comeback in 1996 – again with Yamaha – was stupendous. He just missed out on the title after a classic battle with teammate Niall Mackenzie.

His performance led to another stint on World Superbike duty with Suzuki in 1997–8, which netted him three more podiums. He spent 1999 'freelancing' as he held out for a competitive ride. During this year he won the World Supersport 600 race at Donington Park for Belgarda Yamaha and rode Kenny Roberts's Modenas KR3 in GPs until breaking his pelvis, earning praise from the great man himself for his racing guile. Jamie currently rides for the Belgarda squad, and after a couple of seasons battling in the top three it may not be long before the rider from Huddersfield finally brings home the world title his talent and courage deserve.

Jamie Whitham, paddock joker and as fast as they come.
(Mark Wernham)

The years 1992–5 were to be lean times for Suzuki on the race scene. In World Superbike there wasn't a factory effort, and private GSX-Rs were getting nowhere. In the UK Team Grant disappeared at the end of 1992 and the SPRs of 1994 were not seen at the highest levels of British racing. Only in the US did the GSX-R barely hang on to its respectability, thanks to the skills of the riders and Yoshimura. The arrival of the liquid-cooled machine in 1993 helped Turkington win the Supersport 750 class, which Tom Kipp made a back-to-back win a year later. In the Superbike class, Yoshimura ran Thomas Stevens and Donald Jacks for 1993, but a lack of test time and development kept them away from the winners' circle. For 1994, Stevens was joined by Kipp, but despite winter development giving the bikes more mid-range, the best Stevens could manage was still only ninth overall. 1995 saw the return of that old campaigner Merkel, who joined Stevens in the team. Highlight of the year was third for Merkel at Mid Ohio. In Supersport Merkel was again the main man for Suzuki, but a crash in the final race at Firebird, Arizona, left the Californian with career-ending injuries, which meant he finished second in the series. It was a sad end to Merkel's illustrious career and the end of the racing road for the old double-cradle frame GSX-R.

Tales of endurance

As the GSX-R750 was able to trace its direct ancestry to the GS1000R and the XR41, it was obvious that in its turn the GSX-R would find its way into Endurance racing. The GSX-R750 made its Endurance debut in April of 1985 at the non-championship round of Le Mans, coming first and second. In first place was a privateer French team (the French love Endurance racing) while the factory effort, Dominique Meliand's Suzuki Endurance Race Team (SERT), which was also French, came second, with riders Herve Moineau and

Many of the early 'nineties Endurance GSX-Rs featured this frame design, which was considerably beefier than the standard machine. This is a 1993 works bike. (Mark Wernham)

Richard Hubin. Moineau was already a double world champion, taking the title in 1980 – when the series had just been awarded its world championship status – and in 1983 aboard the GS1000R, a machine which shared many design attributes with the GSX-R750. Over the following years the French team and its riders would stoke up patriotic fervour to make the Suzuki a popular machine in France, with the gloriously sexy Minolta-backed bikes of 1988 and 1989 providing the gorgeous silhouette for the GSX-Rs of the late 1980s and early 1990s.

Moineau would take the title twice more with the Suzuki GSX-R750 in 1987 (with Bruno le Bihan) and in 1988 (with Thierry Crine). The second of the two victories was against considerable factory opposition. Later, as the shortcomings of the double-cradle frame became apparent, the factory machines used by SERT and seen at the Suzuka Eight-Hour featured heavily braced headstocks and top rails which were made out of grotesquely huge box section aluminium – nothing like the stock frame at all. With the switch to water-cooled motors in 1992, the SERT team had a mathematical chance of the championship against the Kawasaki France ZXR750 of Carl Fogarty and

Pete Goddard would win the 1997 Endurance title and the 1996 Australian Superbike title for Suzuki. His experience would lead to a stint with the World Superbike team in 1998.
(Mark Wernham)

Terry Rymer, but a victory for the Brits in Johor meant that the title went to Kawasaki. When the beam-framed WT debuted in 1996, Rymer was now riding for SERT, and a strong showing throughout the year showed the new bike's potential. It was in 1997 that the title went back to Suzuki once more, with Peter Goddard and Doug Polen on board, both riders with strong links with Suzuki and immense experience. Two years later SERT would win again, this time with Rymer back on board alongside Christian Lavielle and with more than a little help from Jamie Whitham.

Two titles on the trot for Suzuki came from the unlikely source of a privateer team, as in 2000 the superb British-based privateer team of Whirley Phase One took the championship. In 2001 the Wim Motors Honda VTR took the Superbike World Endurance title, with the SERT team taking the Endurance World Cup for Superproduction machines (that's four-cylinders up to 1,000cc and 1,200cc twins). With rules favouring the big 1,000cc machines, and considering the dominance of the GSX-R1000 (it won seven of eight races), surely it's only a matter of time before the championship is won by a GSX-R again?

British privateers Whirley Phase One took the World Endurance title in 2000. (Mark Wernham)

The 1996 GSX-R750WT:
'Built to win'

April 8th 1993 proved to be a momentous day in the history of the GSX-R750, for this was the day that Suzuki's top brass met at Suzuki Motor Corporation headquarters in Hamamatsu and came up with the decision to build a new generation of lightweight, high-performance 750cc sports bike. Suzuki wanted something that would continue and develop the firm's excellent record in World Endurance racing, while at the same time giving them a platform with which to launch a serious assault on the World Superbike championship, a series the firm desperately wanted to win. Out on the street, they also needed to produce a supersports 750 machine capable of taking on the best that the opposition could throw at them.

The people gathered around the table knew their current 750 supersports model, the GSX-R750WP, could not do the job, nor could it be achieved by simple development, suffering as it did from two major and inherent drawbacks. Firstly, the water-cooled motor which had debuted just 12 months earlier in 1992 with the GSX-R750WN was seen by its relatively poor racing results to be what it was – simply a stop-gap to better things. Secondly, those classic lines of the double cradle aluminium

It was a winner from the start. Phil West on the 750WT.
(Suzuki)

frame, which had been a signature for the GSX-R in various capacity guises since the GSX-R750F was unveiled back at Cologne in 1984, had to go.

The double cradle had served the GSX-R well, but had hamstrung it since the

introduction of the aluminium beam frame which the opposition's machines had been using since the late 1980s. The beam frame meant that you could make the whole chassis stiffer, stronger, and lighter, and you could move the engine around or tilt it forward in the frame

to get the best possible weight distribution, while leaving the maximum space for an airbox and its ancillaries, which in turn meant that you could maximise the efficiency of your chosen motor.

So, everyone around the table that day knew what had to be done: the 750 super-sport machine as Suzuki, and possibly the world, knew it had to undergo a complete revision. One thing they could draw on was the name. The GSX-R moniker had served Suzuki well for the best part of a decade. It was a name that meant performance, at all costs.

Haruo Terado was group leader for Suzuki's Motorcycle Engineering Design Department and he was one of those sitting around that table back in April 1993. He recalls: 'In 1993 many manufacturers released new 750cc models. This made it necessary to create a new generation of the GSX-R750 with that heritage.' The heritage was very important. Far from being just another streetbike, the original GSX-R750 invented the term 'race-replica' in the dictionary of motorcycling, as well as providing a concise and accurate definition. The Suzuki engineers in charge of that original project called the concept 'Born on the circuit, back to the circuit.' The original GSX-R750, based on a successful works race bike, had in turn become a successful race machine in its own right, although success with the water-cooled WN and WP machines was proving much harder to come by.

Throughout a decade's worth of model refinements, the original GSX-R750 had also became a huge sales success for Suzuki. It had also formed the basis for the Suzuki Cup Series, which transformed racing and gave rise to a new class of professional and semi-professional road racers all over the world. And it inspired an entire generation of copy-cat machines built by competing manufacturers. It

was inevitable that given enough time, the other motorcycle manufacturers would get it right, and so it was that in early 1993 the GSX-R750, while still selling, no longer stood out as the top performer in the increasingly competitive 750cc high-performance motorcycle arena. So, keeping that illustrious name alive was a start as well as being important for the identity and nature of this new machine – if only they had a machine they could base certain key components on.

In early 1993 one man who was a key player in the early development of the GSX-R, Kevin Schwantz, was doing rather well in 500cc GPs. Schwantz – ever the darling of road racing fans – had put the early models of the GSX-R750 on the racing map, and in recent years he had been the only man to make the fickle Suzuki RGV500 Gamma two-stroke competitive on a season-long basis. He was a colourful character in the GP paddock. He matched a quick wit and win-or-crash attitude to his natural and almost unearthly talent for riding a race bike. The combination of all these factors had seen his popularity soar since his four-stroke racing days. But in the years since joining the GP circus full-time in the late 1980s, Schwantz had been finding it hard to mount a consistent season-long campaign. Problems with the demanding RGV500, and Schwantz's insistence on riding around these problems at ten-tenths capacity with only a win on his mind, led to the inevitable – crashes and injury – while his main title rival Wayne Rainey was Mr Consistent, which won him three back-to-back titles in 1990–2.

In 1993, though, it was different. Schwantz had a machine which at last was equal, if not the superior, to the Yamaha YZR500 and Honda NSR500, thanks in no small part to new-for-1992 crew chief Stuart Shenton. He also had a new attitude to racing: if you have to finish fifth once every so often to win a title, so be it. By April of that year winter testing had shown the 1993 RGV500 to be a major leap forward over the 1992 machine, and it won first time out in Schwantz's hands at the season opener at Eastern Creek in Australia. Here, then, was a machine on which to base the new GSX-R750. It was almost like a distant relation of the old two-stroke RG500 marrying into the direct bloodline of the GSX-R750 to make one hell of a thoroughbred motorcycle.

This was a radical step, and one which was in reality taking the race-replica concept to a much higher level, by using the RGV500 as the baseline for an entirely new GSX-R750. As the months of early development meetings wore on, it was clear that, in terms of sheer performance, the RGV500 represented the finest machine Suzuki had ever made. So it became clear to them that they shouldn't settle for the conventional, normal practice of refining previous models. Instead, they would start with the absolute best in terms of performance, handling, and light weight, and build a 750cc four-stroke motor to go in it, a motor which would stick to the principles applied to the original heart of the very first GSX-R750. Surely, this would result in a production 750 like no other.

By October 1993, Kevin Schwantz had ridden the RGV500 to the 500cc World Championship, albeit under the dark cloud of his title rival Wayne Rainey suffering career-ending injuries at Misano, which led to the Californian being paralysed. But Schwantz was champion and the message was clear – the 1993 RGV500 *was most definitely* the bike on which to base the new GSX-R. Work on the 1996 Suzuki GSX-R750 was by now well under way.

Haruo Terado remembers the original goals for the next generation GSX-R750. He recalls: 'When we started development work in the spring of 1993 we decided that the best way to achieve a truly high performance, next generation motorcycle was to combine Kevin Schwantz's 1993 factory machine, the RGV Gamma, with a light weight and compact four-stroke 750cc power plant. The main goals were to be "light weight", "fast", and "easy to use". Weight was especially important since it directly affects acceleration and braking as well as fuel efficiency.' Terado says that at the time, it was simply a case of giving the project engineers the basic idea (the RGV500) and some target figures to hit and be mindful of what the GSX-R750 had done in the past. 'The foremost aim for the GSX-R750, therefore, was to keep the whole machine as light as possible,' he says. 'Right from the start of development we established a target weight of 179 kilos (393.8lb), as well as a power-to-weight ratio of 1.398 kilos per horsepower. The original oil-cooled GSX-R750 which we introduced way back in 1985 was, compared to other models at the time, much, much lighter and higher performing. It received much acclaim and maintained a strong popularity for such a very long time. But as often happens in motorcycling, many new different performance demands were added and in response to those demands, weight increased little by little and so that after some years the bike had become significantly heavier. We felt that we really had to re-focus on the original "light weight" concept of this bike. Usually we start development by deciding specifications in detail, but in the case of the 1996 GSX-R750, we simply established the basic concept and the two target figures – everything else we left to our engineers.'

The gestation period for this birth from table-top discussion to Misano track launch was to be more than two years.

From silhouette to superbike

Engineers on the 1996 Suzuki GSX-R750 superbike programme wanted to make this machine the finest 750 superbike ever. Loosely, their design goals were: on the track this bike had to be a race winner, a machine capable of winning World Superbike and Endurance series; while in street trim, the new bike was to be the lightest, best performing, best handling machine in its class. Normally market research would determine the specifications and design features of new motorcycles. But in this case the stated primary goals of racing success and street dominance guided the entire engineering process, while the final details and specifications of the completed motorcycle would be left to the engineers. Only once before had engineers and not marketing men been given such a free hand. This had been when Honda produced the mighty CBR900RR FireBlade back in 1992.

The fundamentals for racing success were simple enough. The new GSX-R750 would need a powerful engine and a slippery shape for high top speed. It would need light weight for quick acceleration. And a rigid chassis with the right wheelbase, geometry, and suspension for rapid transitions from upright to full lean, full throttle to maximum braking, as well as the ability to sustain high cornering speeds. The engineers started with the basic dimensions and elements of the RGV500. The wheelbase, the overall length and height, even down to the RGV's twin-tube diamond aluminium alloy frame and aerodynamic shape. Everything was scrutinised.

Pretty soon Suzuki realised they needed a fully integrated approach to designing this bike. Traditionally, one team produced the motor and another the chassis, but the project leaders realised the targets for the new GSX-R would demand a 'fully integrated' design philosophy.

So, the project started with a clean sheet of paper and had to be designed as a complete package, not an assembly of parts.

Creating a package as small and compact as the RGV500 required a new take on the design and layout of the 750cc four-cylinder, four-stroke production motorcycle engine. The overall engine design goals were easily stated, with racing success topping the list. Compared to existing powerplants, the new engine had to deliver more power than the previous model's engine as well as more than its rivals in the 750 class, and possibly challenge even the power outputs being seen from 900cc engines. This had to be allied to excellent reliability in a compact, lightweight design. Put simply, the new GSX-R750 needed a production racing engine performance with streetbike longevity. Such was the challenge set before engine designer Masahiro Nishikawa.

Displacement was the easy part, 750cc being the limit for World Superbike and Endurance racing for inline fours, and inline four was the chosen configuration because historically this was what Suzuki did best. This motor would also be a short-stroke high revving beast. Max rpm would be 13,500 and the bore and stroke would be 72 x 46mm, the same dimensions as Yamaha's YZF750 – which at the time was probably the best 750 on the road – and also identical to Honda's RC30 production racer.

The valve train would be double overhead cams with bucket tappets and four valves per cylinder, the best combination for power-producing valve area without needless complexity and unnecessary mechanical friction. Two valve springs control each valve, and valve lash is adjusted with replaceable shims underneath the bucket tappets. The engineers

Suzuki's 1996 750 featured SRAD, or Suzuki Ram Air Direct. The system rams air into a pressurised airbox and boosts power at speed. (Suzuki)

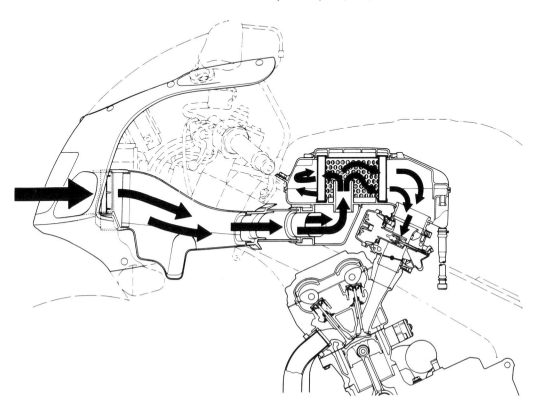

decided to revert to a short-stroke design delivering high, peakpower-producing rpm along with slower piston speeds for less mechanical friction and more durability. Bore and stroke were set at 72 x 46mm.

Then the engineers moved on to the fuel-burning heart of the engine, the combustion chamber. Developing efficient combustion and effective cylinder charging is the key to mid-range power and combustion chamber shape is a critical factor. It isn't just a numbers game and it isn't as simple as saying that a certain valve angle or compression ratio or combustion chamber volume is the best. Instead, it's a matter of getting the combination right, of finding the ideal specifications and relationships to make an engine reach its full potential. In the case of the new GSX-R750, the numbers all came together

with a compact, 15cc combustion chamber, a flat-topped piston, 11.8:1 compression ratio, an included valve angle of 29°, and a short, downdraft intake port.

The engine had to be small, compact, and light, as well as efficient and powerful. Figuring out how to make an engine narrower and lighter had been done before. But thanks to basic changes in the engine layout, the new GSX-R750's crankcases are significantly shorter front to rear compared to the previous model's, allowing a shorter wheelbase and concentrating engine mass closer to the centre of the wheelbase, which in turn aids handling. The gearbox shafts are relocated from directly behind the crankshaft to below and behind it, on a separate split in the crankcases. The new GSX-R750's gearbox shafts are closer to the

crankshaft centreline, and the crankshaft has a smaller primary gear. Production realities usually dictate that the primary gear machined into the crankshaft be large enough for a gear-cutting tool to clear the adjacent counterweight. But the new GSX-R750 uses a bolt-on counterweight eliminating a production-imposed design constraint and allowing the smaller primary gear needed to make the engine more compact.

Internally Suzuki decided to replace the conventional pressed-in cast-iron liners with SCEM (Suzuki Composite Electro-chemical Material) nickel-silicon-carbide plating applied directly to the aluminium cylinders. This allowed bore centres to be moved 5mm closer together. With these changes, the crankshaft could be shorter and more rigid, and mechanical friction was reduced. The closely-spaced bore centres also made it possible to make the intake ports straight. Because the cam chain didn't run up the middle of the engine, the intake ports didn't have to turn outward to feed the outside cylinders.

Suzuki engineers had more than 20 years' experience with SCEM cylinder linings, starting with the aluminium alloy rotor housing of the 1974 RE-5 rotary engine. SCEM-coated cylinders are lighter, more compact and more durable than cylinders with conventional iron liners. The heat expansion rate of SCEM-coated aluminium alloy cylinders is a better match to the heat expansion rate of pistons, and SCEM-coated cylinders transfer heat better, reducing piston and ring wear. SCEM-coated cylinders have been proven in the worst possible off-road and road racing conditions, and are used on RGV500 race machines and RM competition dirt bikes.

Making the whole motor compact also helped to make it lighter, and remember, the design parameters set by Suzuki top brass to the development team were tough. Still, they managed to cut a lot of fat off the new motor. Compared to the 1995 model, the 1996 engine's cylinder head was 1.5kg (3.3lb) lighter, while the cylinder assembly was 2kg (4.4lb) lighter and the crankshaft 1kg (2.2lb) lighter. Other changes were made to directly reduce weight, such as simplifying cooling system hose routing and eliminating an external water pipe, saving a further kilo. Because the new engine's crankshaft is so much narrower, it was possible to relocate the alternator to the left end of the crankshaft without reducing ground clearance during hard cornering. This also eliminated the separate alternator drive gears and housing and saved a further 2kg. Even with the relocated alternator, the engine was still extremely narrow for the time, measuring 469mm (18.5in) at the widest part of the crankcases. Extra weight saving measures included a clutch cover made of magnesium alloy instead of aluminium alloy (this saved 250gm, or 8.8oz). Magnesium was also used for the valve cover, starter clutch cover, and the engine sprocket cover in a further bid to lose excess weight. The alternator was 922gm (2lb) lighter, using newly developed, smaller and thinner magnets. The starter motor used the same type of new magnets and was 453gm (1lb) lighter.

All the gases developed by the new motor were captured and expelled by a single-wall, stainless steel exhaust system with an aluminium alloy silencer. This new exhaust also saved another 1.6kg (3.5lb), making the new GSX-R750's entire engine package 9kg (19.8lb) lighter than its predecessor.

For most of the early 1990s, Kawasaki had pioneered the use of ram-air, a system where the air is forced at speed into a pressurised airbox, which when fed into the carbs is burnt more efficiently. At speed, this could lead to an increase of as much as five per cent more power in the output of an engine. Suzuki wanted to do a similar thing with the new GSX-R, so developed

This cutaway of the motor shows its compact design. What you can't see is the amount of power it produces – 126bhp. (Suzuki)

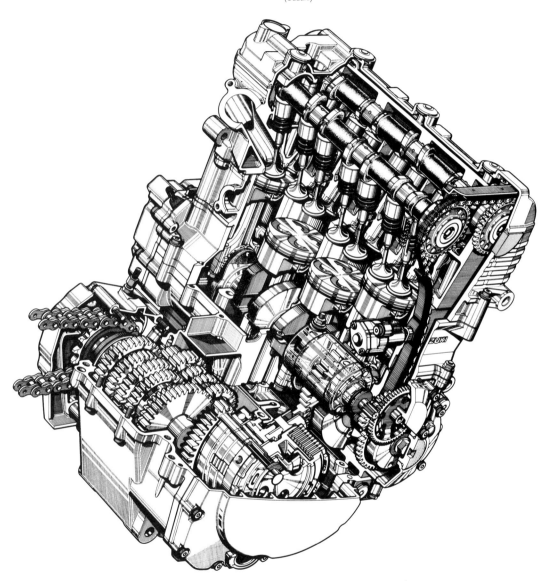

their own induction system known as Suzuki Ram-Air Direct, or SRAD. SRAD induction utilised electronically enhanced carburation, with air fed from two large scoops either side of the headlights. Ducts then routed the air through the frame spars to feed the pressurised air through three air chambers into the airbox, and then into

smaller, filter-equipped vent tubes to equalise the pressure inside the carburettors. The carbs were big 39mm Mikunis, featuring a new design.

Normally, such a large bore carb would give high rpm power, but ultimately sacrifice torque and mid-range oomph. Carb sizes are always a balance between what is best for the street, or

for homologation regs. But the 1996 GSX-R750's down-draft CV-type carburettors featured a unique new slide shape and a new vacuum chamber pressure control system to improve throttle response and driveability. The reshaped semi flat-slide was streamlined with a bevelled face, reducing turbulence and smoothing air flow through the venturi, making the fuel/air mixture more consistent throughout the rpm range. A conventional CV-type carburettor's slide is raised by the vacuum produced by the pressure differential between the vacuum chamber, which is usually vented to the atmosphere, and the carb venturi, only indirectly linking slide lift, engine rpm, and throttle position. The new system directly matched carburettor intake area to engine speed and throttle position, which all added up to that important feeling of driveability. A solenoid valve rapidly switched between vent lines leading to the pressurised airbox (high pressure) and to the manifold (low

pressure), regulating the pressure in the vacuum chamber to obtain the desired piston slide lift. At low engine rpm, slide lift was limited. At high engine rpm, slide lift was dramatically increased. This system was controlled by the electronic engine management black box, which monitored throttle angle and engine rpm sensors. The black box controlled the ignition system and a low pressure fuel pump.

The 1996 GSX-R750 used a digital electronic ignition system. Extensive dynamometer testing led to separate ignition timing maps for cylinders one and four and cylinders two and three, compensating for minute combustion variables caused by differences in cylinder running temperatures.

When it was all put together, the compact new GSX-R750 engine produced significantly more horsepower (a claimed 126bhp) and weighed 9kg (19.8lb) less than the previous model's engine.

And a new chassis to match

When it came to designing the new GSX-R750's chassis, the engineers faced several crucial factors. They had to wrap a light, rigid frame around the new, compact engine and its SRAD ram-air induction and downdraft intake system. The finished chassis also had to have a small frontal area for less drag, with plenty of ground clearance at maximum lean. For perfect handling, the mass also had to be concentrated in the centre of a short wheelbase. And we're talking about a *very* short wheelbase here. At 1,400mm (55.1in), the 1996 GSX-R750's wheelbase was actually slightly shorter than the RGV500's and that of the hot 600 of the time, Kawasaki's ZX-6R (1,415mm), let alone the 750 competition, and it also featured a steep 24° of rake.

The GSX-R750's main frame spars were welded together using pieces stamped out of aluminium alloy sheet, the same rigid, state-of-the-art construction used to build the frame of the RGV500. Die-cast aluminium alloy sections carrying the steering head bearings and swingarm pivot shaft were welded to the spars. The engine mounts were forged aluminium alloy, and the cross-brace was an extrusion. A bolt-on rear sub-frame was made of extruded aluminium alloy tubing. The assembled frame had twice the torsional rigidity of the previous model's had yet weighed more than 2kg (4.4lb) less.

Suzuki had to mate this stiff chassis to the best suspension and braking components they could. At the front, they chose to use

The 1996 machine was available in the traditional blue and white as well as this 'anthracite'. Early GSX-R750WTs were spotted testing in the US in late summer of 1995. (Suzuki)

chunky 43mm inverted front forks featuring a wide range of spring preload, rebound damping, and compression damping adjustments, although thankfully not in such a bewildering range of settings as on previous GSX-R models. The steering stem and several internal fork components – including the cartridge tubes and cartridge bottom end caps – were made from aluminium alloy instead of steel, making the 1996 model's forks 780gm (1.7lb) lighter than those used on the 1995 model.

The aluminium alloy swingarm combined a cast pivot section with extruded arms and braces and had 12 per cent more torsional rigidity than the previous swinger. The swingarm pivot point also featured replaceable

Roland Brown on the 'other' 1996 launch colour. Unsurprisingly, the Moonstone option was not as popular as the striking corporate Suzuki Blues. (Roland Brown)

inserts for adjustment of the pivot point itself –
more than a mere nod to the bike's sporting
pretensions. Rear ride-height could be
adjusted at the upper shock mount, and
the adjustable Showa rear shock with piggy-
back oil reservoir was 200gm (7oz) lighter
than the remote reservoir shock it replaced.
The rear shock linkage was smaller and, along
with aluminium alloy link rods, saved another
half a kilo (1.1lb). To further illustrate the
lengths to which Suzuki's engineers went to
save weight, even the spacer between the
swingarm pivot bearings was made of
aluminium alloy instead of the steel used for
previous models.

The hollow front and rear axle shafts were
larger and more rigid, while thinner casting
walls and aluminium alloy bearing spacers
made both wheels weigh less, the front being
400gm (14.1oz) lighter and the rear 900gm
(2lb). Even the tyres were lighter and yet
bigger, with the 190/50 rear larger than the 180
used previously, but actually weighing the
same thanks to a new construction. This
attention to detail helped bring the overall
weight down and down. Simpler engine
mounting saved 900gm (2lb), integrating the
battery box into the plastic rear mudguard
another half a kilo (1.1lb), a tubular sidestand
in place of a forged one saved 350gm
(12.3oz), smaller rider and passenger footpeg
brackets saved 740gm (1.6lb), eliminating
plastic frame covers and airbox side covers
saved 750gm (1.7lb), and a simpler front
mudguard saved another 400gm (14.1oz).
Small amounts, but they all added up and
were then taken away. All together, the new
GSX-R750's chassis was more rigid, more
compact, and almost 9kg (19.8lb) lighter than
its predecessor.

The brakes on the new bike had to more
than match that impressive motor. The outside
diameter of the front brake discs was 10mm
larger, but weight was saved as the actual
discs were thinner, measuring 4.5mm instead
of 5mm. The biggest reason the larger discs
were actually 230gm (8.1oz) *lighter* was
due to the inside diameter being larger as
well, with the brake pad swept area moved
outward.

A new, sleek shape

The clothes in which to wrap the new GSX-
R750 had to work on three counts. They had
to maximise the advantage given by the new,
powerful motor and lighter chassis while
looking attractive to potential customers,
and at the same time had to still be
unmistakably GSX-R.

Wind tunnel testing helped adapt the
aerodynamic shape of the RGV500's fairing
and bodywork to the specific dimensions of
the 1996 GSX-R750. When the design work
and testing were completed, the GSX-R750's
aggressively slanted fairing nose extended
just 125mm (4.92in) ahead of the front
wheel spindle. The longer front mudguard
wrapped farther around the leading edge of
the front tyre. The fairing itself extended
rearward to just ahead of the rear tyre.
And a delta-shaped fin just ahead of the
rear tyre deflected air flow, as well as water
running off the bottom of the fairing in wet
conditions, redirecting it around each side of
the spinning rubber hoop. The wind tunnel
testing also confirmed a surprisingly simple
but almost universally overlooked discovery.
With the tail piece shaped just right, the
turbulence behind the motorcycle could be
dramatically reduced, the air stream

smoothly detaching and flowing downward behind the seat. Instead of leaving a turbulent, top-speed-reducing wake ready to draft a following rider forward, the new tail section smoothes the air flow behind to help the GSX-R750 reach higher speeds and hopefully escape competitors on the racetrack. What it ended up looking like was a smooth tail unit almost heading towards a pointed, wasp-like sting.

The influence of the wind-tunnel testing could even be seen in equipment used only on the street. The indicators (called turn signals over the pond) were rounded and sleek for less drag, and the headlight assembly – unmistakably GSX-R, utilising the trademark twin headlights – fitted flush into the fairing nose. Suzuki engineers paid attention to making street equipment lighter as well. The electronic speedometer incorporated a liquid crystal display (LCD) odometer system and was 350gm (12.3oz) lighter than an equivalent mechanical unit. Eliminating the mechanical speedometer drive saved another 210gm (7.4oz). The headlight lens was also plastic instead of glass, cutting a further 680gm (1.5lb) of fat. The wiring harness was shortened and reorganised to concentrate and centralise electrical components, saving a further 120gm (4.2oz). Combined with reductions in engine and chassis weight, the road equipment weight savings made the new GSX-R about 20kg (44lb) lighter than the 1995 GSX-R750S it replaced.

As if to accentuate the race-ready feel of the new GSX-R further, the GSX-R750T featured several racetrack-inspired features to make maintenance easier. For example, the wheel spacers were captive, staying in place instead of falling onto the ground when the wheels were removed – a nice touch for club racers, endurance racers, and WSB

mechanics alike. The engine oil filter was also mounted at a 90° angle on the front of the engine, for easier replacement. The fairing was held on with fewer fasteners and the number of different fastener sizes was reduced. The fuel tank was hinged at the rear and swung upward to allow easier access to the air cleaner and spark plugs. A handy fuel-tank prop-rod was stowed in the tailpiece luggage compartment so to facilitate easy maintenance. The pillion compartment could be covered by the top of the tail section for solo riding, or by the passenger seat for two-up riding. Both tail section cover and the passenger seat were standard equipment, so you didn't have to splash out for a single-seat cowling.

It was obvious that the Suzuki was – like its predecessor all those years ago – a real race replica. But Suzuki knew that it couldn't make the Suzuki too razor sharp or focused. Therefore, to help rider comfort, the 1996 GSX-R750 featured an improved riding position, with slightly higher handlebars and slightly lower footpegs than the 750S, but without sacrificing the requirements of the racing crouch.

When the time came for the launch of this new machine, late in 1995 at the Misano Adriatico circuit in Italy, Suzuki billed it as 'A race-replica like no other, a motorcycle built to win.' It was a brave boast, but at least they'd hit those targets. When the first bikes were lined up in the Misano pit lane for the waiting journalists, the new Suzuki GSX-R750 weighed 179kg (394.6lb) and delivered a power-to-weight ratio of 1.4kg (3.1lb) per horsepower. Its size and shape came straight from the Grand Prix circuit but was most definitely a four-stroke GSX-R.

And it was to take the race-replica concept to an entirely new level.

The new GSX-R750 shocks the world

Press reaction at the Misano launch was nothing short of phenomenal. Many said that here at last was a machine with the performance to take on the Honda FireBlade, something with a much stronger sporting character. And pretty much everyone came away with a positive reaction to the new GSX-R.

Phil West from the UK's *Bike* magazine had a long career riding GSX-Rs and for him this was the finest ever. Following his test for the magazine, he wrote: 'Imagine a 750 sports scalpel, so focused and compact it's not only the smallest and lightest inline-four 750 ever built, it's also dinkier and daintier than every inline-four 600 too… Imagine a 750 that brakes and slices into turns as sharply as a 400 supersports, yet powers out of them like only a 12,000rpm 120bhp+ 750 racer can. Now try to conjure up a machine that, in one package, combines the very latest and best of four-cylinder sportsbike design – drawn from every corner of Japan: a frame inspired by Yamaha's Deltabox, power-to-weight figures that best even the awesome Honda FireBlade and a powerplant that mixes Kawasaki Ram-Air with peerless Suzuki sheen. Sound too much to imagine? Then don't, the dreaming is over. The bike is the new GSX-R750.'

Freelance journalist Alan Cathcart agreed, writing in monthly road-race mag *RPM*: 'It changes direction so fast, yet so precise is the steering – but it's nimble without being twitchy. You hardly need to move a muscle to make it turn into an apex. The Suzuki's handling is so neutral. It's just that everything happens so quickly – just like on a works 500GP bike. But the real peach is that fabulous motor, undoubtedly the best four-cylinder 750cc motorcycle engine

yet put into production. It'll pull cleanly from as low as 2,000 rpm which with a 13,000 redline gives it a pretty outrageous powerband.'

Motor Cycle News were quick to get hold of the 1996 GSX-R750 and its major rival, the new Honda CBR900RR FireBlade, to see which was best. The test took place in mid-January as soon as examples of both hit the UK showrooms. Tester Chris Moss went on both continental launches for the Suzuki and the Honda, so he had a good idea of the strong points of both machines as he tested them in the murk of Northamptonshire in January. Eventually he couldn't separate them, the Honda winning votes for its more civilised nature and user-friendliness, while the Suzuki had a hard-edged race bike quality that really made it at home on the track. He said: 'As a pure focused sports bike nothing in the 750 class can match the new GSX-R and nor can the new big-bore 'Blade. It's the greatest pure sportsbike Japan has ever built. If ultimate performance is what you need, the Suzuki is the new leader of the gang. While Honda has toned down the FireBlade, Suzuki has done everything it could to maintain the famed hard-edged GSX-R reputation.'

Further accolades awaited the GSX-R on the other side of the Atlantic. In *Cycle World* the Suzuki GSX-R750 won the 'Ultimate Sportbike Challenge', beating both the Honda FireBlade and the Ducati 916. It wrote: 'The Suzuki GSX-R750 is the closest thing yet to a street-legal GP bike. No, the Gixxer isn't perfect, but it picks up where the CBR900RR FireBlade left off in the power-to-weight department. Not only is the GSX-R impressive for a 750, it also outperformed the 900RR in nearly every aspect of our

Phil West went on the launch for the new GSX-R and loved it. The machine was back at the top of the 750 pile and was threatening the likes of the Honda FireBlade for top sportsbike honours. (*Bike* magazine)

performance testing.' The US's *Sport Rider* saw Suzuki's 750 take top honours in shoot-outs with both the Yamaha YZF750R and the new for 1996 Kawasaki ZX-7R. It also later went on to take the honours in the 1996 Bike of the Year poll ahead of the Ducati 916, Honda CBR900RR FireBlade, and Honda CBR600.

Superbike magazine's Gordon Ritchie was on the Misano launch, but wanted to get a real-world opinion on the new bike. Getting hold of one of the first of the new GSX-R750Ts in the country in early 1996, he got together a jury of five sportsbike riders (three of whom were committed GSX-R fanatics) and let them loose on the latest Suzuki. All were mightily impressed. Ritchie explains: 'There was one feature that everyone complained about on the new GSX-R.

You can't see the clocks. And that's it. Every single rider who threw a leg over this year's GSX-R was really affected by just one short ride on it. The last bikes to have this sort of an affect on people were the Honda FireBlade and the Ducati 916. Like both of these bikes, the 1996 GSX-R750 is a mould breaker and an instant classic. Don't take my word for it though... just ask these five.'

In the same issue the new machine was speed tested and dynoed for the first time and subjected to British roads and weather at their very worst. It was a measure of the bike that it still impressed. Despite a damp Bruntingthorpe, the GSX-R750T still loped through the lights at 167mph (269kph) and set a 10.57s quarter mile time. On the dyno it got an impressive back wheel figure of 121bhp (90.26kW) at 11,200rpm, 6bhp (4.48kW) more

than the previous year's Honda FireBlade.

In his test, which was headlined 'Fire Extinguisher', John Cantlie was gibbering in his praise. 'Sorry everyone, but it's bike journalist ranting time. The new GSX-R750 is the one. This is the bike that's going to sell out, that's going to be THE track machine, that's going to be the subject of a thousand pub hero stories. The GSX-R is so light and fast it makes every 750 ever made instantly dull in terms of out-and-out sportsbike riding. It breathes fire and brimstone out of each lightweight nut and drilled bolt. It farts napalm out of the alloy exhaust and it is genuinely, utterly barking. If you think you are good at riding, you're in for a shock. The GSX-R750T is faster than you, better than you and will spit you off as soon as look at you. In their quest to create the ultimate sportsbike perhaps Suzuki has taken it a titchy bit too far. The new GSX-R really is a bit of an animal.'

Later that year *Superbike* undertook two major tests. One was to decide the Sportsbike of the Year for 1996, the other was to take all the road-going machines from the World Superbike series and see which one was best. In Sportsbike of the Year the line-up of Yamaha's TRX850, YZF600, and YZF1000 Thunderace took on the new Honda CBR900RR FireBlade, the Kawasaki ZX-7R, and the new GSX-R in a track and road based test. The Suzuki came second behind the

Kawasaki – thanks to the very same balls-out attitude which first endeared the bike to them. 'The Suzuki is so crazy that it couldn't win,' the conclusion read. 'It's fair to say that the Suzuki is the most single-minded road bike any of us have ever ridden, which makes it ecstasy in the right places and agony in the wrong ones. 10,000rpm and 140mph are your two operational parameters with the GSX-R. Once you're there everything else just falls into place, but at human speeds the brakes feel wooden, the lack of mid-range is a menace and the greased-lightning handling tiring work.'

Later that year the Suzuki got its revenge on the ZX-7 by just taking the honours in a *Superbike* magazine battle against the road-going versions of the Ducati 916, Yamaha YZF750, Kawasaki ZX-7R, and Honda RC45.

In 1997 the GSX-R750T became the V, with just colour changes. For the following year, fuel injection would give both the road-going GSX-R750 and its track racing brethren a shot in the arm just when 750cc inline fours were having a tough time on the track and while the road-going 750cc class was becoming a little stagnant. Still, something with a bit more oomph and attitude would be along in time for the turn of the century, to stimulate interest in the 750cc class once more. Unsurprisingly, it would bear the name GSX-R.

1998 GSX-R750W: a shot in the arm

In 1997 the GSX-R750V was leader of the 750 pack and still the only machine to take the fight to the more powerful and bigger capacity Honda CBR900RR FireBlade. But while things were staying still in the 750 market, Suzuki realised that the kettle had to be kept boiling when it came to the GSX-R and its ability to offer itself as an alternative to the likes of the FireBlade. The GSX-R wasn't broke, so it didn't need fixing, but with small, subtle improvements it could mature into a better machine, bit by bit.

The biggest revision was to be in the heart of the motor, to its fuelling. Fuel injection systems had been

around for years on cars, especially performance cars, but bolting such costly and comparatively complex things on a motorcycle was seen for years as a whim and a triumph of marketing over performance. In the early 1990s the majority of machines that featured fuel injection were Bimotas and Ducatis, with the notable exception of the hub-centre steered Yamaha GTS1000A, which, while worthy, was a sales flop. To many, if fuel injection systems were so good and improved performance so much, why weren't the Japanese engineers bolting them on to bikes in the first place? Machines such as Bimota's gorgeously crafted

SB6 and SB7 machines, powered by the GSX-R1100 and water-cooled GSX-R750 motors, proved the point in the hands of motorcycle magazines the world over, as they rarely worked as well as the standard, carburated machines. Until fuel injection could use technology to work as well as, let alone better than carbs in the same very tight space and without prohibitive cost, carbs would win the day. Suzuki decided just after the launch of the 750T in 1996 that this was exactly what they had to do to keep the GSX-R's edge intact for the 1998 season.

Inside the GSX-R750W's fuel injection system, were large 46mm throttle bodies and a two-stage system which monitored water and intake temperatures, outside air temperatures, intake air pressures, throttle position, and engine rpm, to offer the optimal fuel/air mix in both low and high rpm engine regimes. A CDI ignition coil was adopted and the engineers worked on certain internal engine parts to further cut weight. The camshaft position was also revised. Other updates were the inclusion of a much closer ratio gearbox than seen on the previous T and V models. There was also a new, stronger rear shock mount and a slightly taller screen.

Strangely there was no real shouting from Suzuki about the inclusion of the fuel injection system. Compared to the launch of its predecessor, the 750W came on stream very quietly, with no major restyle either, as it looked almost identical to the previous model. The only way anyone less than a technical boffin could tell the machines apart was by looking at the small stencil above the '750' logo of the W, which said 'electronic fuel injection'. Perhaps this very quiet entry into the market, with little or no trumpeting, was done in case the whole thing backfired; or more likely simply to homologate the new fuel injection system for World Superbike racing.

Suzuki needn't have worried. Press reaction wasn't negative at all. In fact many journalists praised the power delivery which came from the addition of fuel injection. *Bike* magazine got to test the 750W at the end of 1997. Kevin Raymond bemoaned the fact that there was no restyle to go with the new fuel injection system, but enjoyed the bike: 'At first sight there's sod-all difference between this year and last year's GSX-R750. Apart from the colour scheme and some subtle graphic changes there's nothing to tell them apart. Paradoxically, all the mods actually make the road bike feel slower, rather than faster than the previous model. It's all in the power delivery. The old model's got an all-or-nothing powerband that leaves you waiting while it gathers its breath, then takes off for the horizon in a searing rush of acceleration, wheelying or wheelspinning all the way. The old GSX-R was a wheelie monster, but not so on the new bike. It's – dare I say it – almost civilized! But it's deceptive, the peak power's there, but its just easier to keep that front end planted, thanks to that smoother power delivery. where the older model gets ready to launch into hyperspace at the touch of a button, the new one winds up like a turbine and gets there first.' Early January saw *Bike* take one of the GSX-Rs down to the South of France along with a new Honda VFR800i, a Ducati 748SPS, and a Kawasaki ZX-7R. It was a pretty diverse range of bikes, but such was the poor state of 750cc supersport machines on offer at the time that *Bike* had to take a 748 V-twin along with an 800cc sports tourer. The result was therefore an interesting one. Martin Child put the 748 and VFR in equal first, as the VFR offered the do-it-all option with the 748 being the ultimate track tool. In second was the GSX-R. 'In a strange way the GSX-R falls between the VFR and 748,' he wrote. 'Where the Honda is a bit lardy and the Ducati too single-minded, the Suzuki offers a range of uses, a degree of comfort and useful things like a pillion seat, U-lock storage and bungee hook points. But yes, the newly fuel-injected missile is still a headbangers dream and it was by far the fastest machine here on test, blitzing through the speed trap at nearly 175mph and scorching to the standing start quarter mile in just 10.7 seconds . Although it failed to make the same impression on each of the four testers, we all agreed it was a top-notch sportster.' One of the testers who did fall for its charms was Steve Westlake. He said: 'The GSX-R is brilliant. It's still got a maniac top end, but the fuel injection gives it more mid-range, so it's less mad than you'd expect. Its firm suspension makes it really planted round the twisties even when the going gets a bit rough. The most surprising thing was that it remained amazingly comfortable even after a whole day in the saddle.'

The 1998 and 1999 750s looked identical to the previous model, but featured fuel injection, operated by two large 46mm throttle bodies. The 1999 machine came in this classy black and metal paint scheme. (Suzuki)

The 750 strikes back: the Y2K GSX-R750Y

As the world moved closer to a new millennium, 750cc Supersports machines were at an all-time low ebb both on the road and on the track. In the UK, few 750s were being sold. In fact, few 750s were even being marketed anymore. Suzuki's 1998 GSX-R750W, which came in the same clothes as the 1996 model, but with fuel injection, was the best machine in its class. It was just that the class itself was so very small.

Where years before Kawasaki had competed with Yamaha, Suzuki, and Honda for honours in this hard-fought class, with machines like the ZXR-750, OW-01, YZF750, GSX-R, VFR750, and RC30, the line-up was now much reduced. Kawasaki had the ZX-7R, which had been selling in steady numbers since its launch in 1996. But since the introduction of this ZXR-750 replacement, Kawasaki had hardly changed a thing on it, save for the palette of colours they annually arrived in. The ZX-7R was – and at the time of writing still is – a great bike. Heavier and less powerful than the GSX-R750T of similar vintage, it had perhaps three great assets. Firstly, it was an attractive machine (especially in green), featuring curves descended from the classic ZXR-750, although now with two huge airscoops either side of separate multi-reflector headlights. Secondly, it was still a superb road machine, inheriting that excellent, planted front-end feel from the ZXRs of old, but without the harsh ride at the rear that the early ZXR750Hs, Js, and to a

The distinctive tail unit of the WT family was gone in place of the much more elegant piece evident in this side-on shot. (Suzuki)

lesser extent Ls suffered from. And if it did have extra pounds to carry compared to its rivals, perhaps that wasn't too bad a thing; this did, after all, make the 7R a much more stable road machine. Its third asset we will deal with later.

Yamaha's 750 offering, the YZF-750, had disappeared in 1998. Despite success in winning three British Superbike titles with Niall Mackenzie and the Cadbury's Boost team in 1996–8, and collecting the 1997 German Pro-Superbike title with Christer Lindholm, as well as experiencing a resurgence in the hands of Noriyuki Haga in World Superbike, in recent years it hadn't sold as well as it should. So, sadly, it disappeared from the streets, quietly and ingloriously, a bizarre antithesis to its glorious swan song on the track.

Meanwhile, Honda's do-it-all workhorse, the VFR750, had now swollen to an 800, leaving the 750 class and gaining extra cee cees along with fuel injection and the removal of any last vestiges of character which the original once had. The VFR was certainly now more of a portly-tourer than a sports-tourer. Which left the Suzuki in a class of just two with the ZX-7R, and it was certainly the top of that class.

One of the reasons that the 750 class had shrunk so dramatically was that the 750s had been attacked and had been engaged in a full-scale war for the last few years. This war was fought on two fronts. Battling from below was the 600cc class, that had moved from being a lightweight, cheaper, sensible option to one which gave the owner the same sort of performance that a 750 delivered – in fact many machines were turning in speeds and performance which bettered some 750s. In 1998, *Bike* magazine timed a Kawasaki ZX-6R at 168.6mph (271.3kph) through the lights. That was faster than any FireBlade or Ducati 916 the magazine had tested before, let alone a 750. It also broke the 11 second standing start quarter mile for the first time for a 600. This class also now had the purposeful looks and kudos that racing gave the bigger machines. Burgeoning Supersport 600 classes at national and international level saw to that.

Catching the 750s in a pincer movement from above were the big-bore supersport machines. These 900 and 1,000cc bikes were no longer the big, fat speed machines of a decade earlier –

Honda's CBR900RR FireBlade had seen to that. Now they were sleeker, lighter, and faster than before. Many were lighter than the supposed pure race 750s and possessed between 10–20bhp more. To demonstrate, Yamaha's YZF-R1 of 1998 weighed in at just 177kg (389.9lb) – 2kg (4.4lb) lighter than the GSX-R750 – and produced a claimed 155bhp (a true real-world figure of around 138bhp as tested by *Bike*), which compared to the Suzuki's claimed 126bhp (118bhp as tested by *Bike* in 1998.) So why the hell would anyone want to buy a 750 anymore?

Remember that third asset that the Kawasaki ZX-7R had? This asset is a race heritage, coming as it did with no little success. The Kawasaki four-stroke superbike lineage came through the ZXR to the ZX-7R and it did pretty well on the racetrack, even compared to the Ducati's dominant V-twins. Green meanie ZXRs, in the hands of Australian Rob Phillis, New Zealander Aaron Slight, and American Scott Russell, had beaten the twins in World Superbike for the last decade, with Russell even claiming the 1993 throne for his own – the only championship for an inline four machine. With the introduction of the 7R for the 1996 season, the wayward talents of Australian Anthony Gobert and his more quietly spoken Kiwi teammate Simon Crafar were following in their wheel tracks, as did successive riders over the years, such as Japan's Akira Yanagawa and Spain's Gregorio Lavilla.

Thanks to this crucible of competition, the ZX-7R earned kudos which came free with a bike that cost the best part of nine grand. All you had to do was watch the numbers of Kawasaki 750s that turned up in race-replica paint schemes. This sort of kudos had eluded other four-cylinder bikes. The RC45 was the main title threat to the Ducatis since 1995, winning the title with the weird and wonderful talents of John Kocinski aboard in 1997, but on the road it was the best part of 20 grand, and by 1999 was withdrawn from Honda dealer lists as the original total for homologation had been sold.

With the OW-02 YZF-R7 of 1999 Yamaha were following Honda's lead in producing expensive limited edition homologation race machines. An exotic, race-developed bike, at the best part of 22 grand it was priced beyond the reach of most bikers' pockets – after all, Yamaha wanted to win the World Superbike title, not take sales from its all-conquering R1. Ironically, as Yamaha went one way, Honda went back in the other, producing the V-twin VTR1000 SP-1, which was built for the road and priced to sell at a tad under £10,000.

So, the manufacturers were supportive of the 750 class, albeit mainly for racing reasons, and with racing 750 fours and 1,000cc twins getting more expensive both for the street and for the track (ironic when you think that Superbike was originally supposed to offer cheaper racing) kudos was still to be found in climbing onto the podium.

For Suzuki this kudos was slow coming. Firstly, the new for 1996 factory team run by Steve and Lester Harris had early stability problems with the bike, before Jamie Whitham gave the bike a handful of podiums in 1997

and 1998 which didn't prove to be enough to stop the factory switching support to the Alstare Racing team. The Corona beer-backed Alstare squad hired a race-winner in the form of Pier-Francesco Chili for the 1999 season and he had some success, but it was *still* slow coming. Guaranteed racing success in World Superbike, it seemed, was only possible if you came equipped with two cylinders or a couple of sandwiches short of a picnic.

For Suzuki it was clear what they must do. Firstly, they must build a road bike that had the performance to beat the 600s handily and then take the fight to the likes of the R1 by offering similar performance, but at less cost and with cheaper insurance. Secondly, they wanted a bike that *really* could have a chance of taking the fight to the V-twins in the World and National Superbike series.

Building a world beater... again

To forge another 750 with the kind of leap in performance enjoyed by its direct predecessor the GSX-R750T meant taking a similar approach. Instead of building a machine from the silhouette of a GP bike, this time Suzuki simply put to good use what it had learned the hard way in World Superbikes to help develop the next generation GSX-R750. Unsurprisingly, two things were needed to beat the 600 and 1,000cc machines: a more powerful motor and a lighter chassis.

Although the motor in the 2000 GSX-R750 looked the same as the 1999 model, it had some big differences deep inside. Inlet and exhaust valves now sat more upright on the cylinder head, which allowed the camshafts to be positioned closer together, which brought the width of the cylinder head down by 9.5mm. These reduced valve angles (12° for the intake valves and 13° for exhaust, both 1° down on the previous model) also resulted in a straighter intake tract and a more compact combustion chamber, with a higher 12:1 compression ratio,

up from 11.8:1. In the bores themselves slid newly designed pistons, which were forged rather than cast, meaning they were lighter and stronger than the previous version. Con-rods also became lighter and more compact, but were also shot-peened for additional strength. The crankshaft had smaller journals and the hollow camshaft had thinner walls, again making a weight saving. The cylinder block and upper crankcase were now cast as one piece, which meant increased strength for less weight. Air injection passageways were cast into the cylinder head, which eliminated the need for external hoses. Nickel-phosphorus silicon carbide coating was applied to the cylinder bores themselves to help heat transfer, which also allowed the use of tighter piston to cylinder clearances. The previous model's steel water to oil cooler was replaced with a lighter aluminium item, while a new four-two-one stainless exhaust system was also lighter than the one it replaced.

Controlling the engine was an all-new 16-bit digital engine management and fuel injection

system, which offered an increase in low and mid-range torque, thanks to the use of twin butterfly valves in each tapered 42mm throttle body. The top butterfly was connected to the throttle and would work in the normal way, but the second was computer controlled and would open progressively to maintain maximum intake velocity. Added to these improvements was a larger SRAD system, which allowed more air into a bigger but lighter airbox. All told, the new mill proved to be lighter and more compact still, being 4kg (8.8lb) lighter, 15mm shorter in length front to rear, 8mm narrower, and a total of 4mm shorter top to bottom than the older engine. All in all this added up to a further five claimed bhp up to 131, which equated to a 'real-world' 120 or so at the rear wheel.

The chassis was perhaps the place where most of the WSB-derived changes came in. The mainframe itself was completely new and was designed and built directly from information gleaned from the firm's WSB racers. The whole chassis package itself was made increasingly stiffer than before, but was now much more compact too, which allowed for a 20mm longer swingarm. This helped increase the wheelbase for the GSX-R from 1,400mm (55.1in) to 1,410mm (55.5in). The long swingarm had been seen before, on racers such as the Yamaha YZR500 and Honda NSR500, and road machines such as the YZF-R1 and the FireBlade. Its purpose was to help get the power down more progressively, with the maximum of traction and without excessive wheelspin. It also helped stability in a straight line. When measured from the bottom of the steering head to the swingarm pivot the frame itself was 10mm shorter than in 1999. It was also lighter, as well as having an improved torsional rigidity to weight ratio, which was up by ten per cent. Design changes and the lighter frame meant that 50.5 per cent of the weight was now over the front wheel, rather than 50 per cent as in the 1999 machine, which helped improve its turning ability just a little. Despite the longer wheelbase, the familiar quick steering of the GSX-R was retained by decreasing the trail by 2mm to 94mm (3.7in), and keeping the steering head angle at 24°.

Suspension-wise, there weren't too many changes. The distance between the two fork legs was reduced by 7mm to reduce the frontal area, to try and narrow down the traditional bulkiness of the across-the-frame-four design. The diameter of the front forks remained 43mm (1.7in), but the length of travel was increased by 5mm to 125mm (4.9in), which lessened the chances of the forks bottoming out under very hard braking or topping out under hard acceleration. At the back, the rising rate Showa monoshock had a main body made of aluminium instead of steel and 25mm shorter than before, while the internal piston size increased by 2mm to 46mm. A new linkage was also used, providing a more linear damping movement.

Braking was accomplished by Tokico four-pots at the front, not six-pots as on the previous model. At the launch Suzuki said they'd developed these four-pots with brake supplier Tokico and found they could get the same braking power with fewer pistons. The eight pistons at the front were now made from aluminium alloy to make them lighter, and thus make the front end easier to turn thanks to less unsprung weight and inertia. Disc sizes remained the same at 320mm at the front and 220mm at the rear. Interestingly, the rear tyre was down from a 190 rear section to a 180. Just as the fashion for six-pot brakes and inverted forks was being bucked, so was the onward trend for wider rubber. Suzuki felt that a 180 rear section offered just as much grip, but with quicker turn-in. All in, the total weight of the new GSX-R was down by 13kg (28.6lb) to 166kg (365.2lb), making it the lightest GSX-R ever.

The styling of the new Y model was simply breathtaking. It was the best-looking large-scale production 750 ever made. Gone was the slightly waspish tail-unit of the previous version, to be replaced by a more elegant, upturned tapering shape. The tank looked similar to the old one, but at the front was an all-new fairing, with a narrower dual-beam headlight, under which sat the mesh-covered SRAD ducts. In the cockpit you had a white-faced tacho and the by now *de rigeur* digital speedo. It looked right – especially in the traditional GSX-R colours of two shades of blue and white – but it still had that traditional GSX-R twin-beam stare with which to take out the opposition.

Schwantz on the 750Y. It was the lightest and most powerful 750 ever built. After years of piling on the pounds, the 750's weight had gone down to just 166kg (365.6lb). (Suzuki)

Press response to the GSX-R750Y

Suzuki wanted to make as much noise as possible over the launch of the new model, so they invited a man along from the GSX-R's early history – Kevin Schwantz. Schwantz certainly enjoyed himself out on the track, wheelying for photographers and making the assembled journos look pretty ordinary on two

wheels. All, it seemed, while he wasn't really trying that hard at all.

John Cantlie from the UK's *Superbike* magazine was knocked out with the new GSX-R's spec-sheet alone: 'Welcome to the GSX-R750Y, the smallest and lightest GSX-R yet built. It weighs an incredible 166 kilos dry. Compare

Martin Child from *Bike* loved the GSX-R. 'The cult of GSX-R
has found a new and very capable president,' he said.
(*Bike* magazine)

that to Yamaha's R6 at 169 or Kawasaki's ZX-6R
at 176 or the Honda CBR600 at 170. Please don't
adjust your screen, those are 600cc dry weights
we're quoting here and the GSX-R is packing
150cc and 30bhp more than they. So to put
things into perspective, imagine an R6 with the
peak power (nearly) of an R1 and you have the
potent package that is the new GSX-R750.'

Martin Child from *Bike* magazine, himself a
GSX-R fanatic, was more than impressed: 'From
the remains of a near extinct class rises a
machine with multiple personalities. As compact
and easy to ride as the class-leading 600s, mid-
range torque of a fit 750 and a top-end power
which – on this first ride – feels like it has the
beating of the new FireBlade and enough to

worry the Yamaha R1. Unlike the R1, the GSX-R
does have certain power zones (calling them
mere powerbands would be an injustice to the
smoothness of the fuel injection). On the Blade
and many other fuel-injected bikes, winding on in
first and second gears can be snatchy as the
motor struggles to match the speed of the bike,
but the Suzuki feels like it's running on well set
up carbs, the power comes in fast and strong
without any jerkiness. In every department the
GSX-R wants to fight with the big boys, even the
motor sounds butch and willing. The GSX-R is as
mental as any model in its 15-year history. The
cult of the GSX-R has just found itself a new and
very capable president.'

Indeed it had. The whole feeling of riding a

The 2000 GSX-R was still the best machine in its class and now had the power to tackle the bigger 1,000cc machines. This is Jon Pearson from *Bike* magazine, giving it the berries. (*Bike* magazine)

GSX-R, whatever its capacity, had to be kept at all costs with the new machine. As well as being refined, better, faster and more nimble it still had to stir the soul.

The UK's *RiDE* magazine specialises in the practical side of motorcycling and in helping people choose the best second-hand buys, which is why they weren't invited to the Misano launch. But even when they got one of the new machines to test, in the grim winter of 2000, they couldn't fail to be impressed. *RiDE*'s Steve Rose explained: 'The new GSX-R750 sounds like a Formula One car on full chat and I find it addictive. The last few days have been spent riding like a prat, at odds with my normal riding style. What is it about GSX-Rs that have that effect? Why do I swagger across the bike park towards it like I'm trying to pick a fight even when I'm only riding home? Because that's the effect GSX-R's have. Those four letters have meant something special for 15 years now. Think of it as a pure-bred street racer, think of it as distilled four-stroke lunacy, think of it as whatever you flippin' well will, just make sure you get a go on one. This is a bike you feel you should arm wrestle before you ride it – and lucky old me has got the first example in the UK to play on for a week.' Rose wasn't disappointed in the performance of the new GSX-R and nor were the many GSX-R, FireBlade, and R1-owning readers who also got to test it during his week with the bike.

Many who rode it either on the launch or back home remarked on the excellence of the new machine's throttle response, especially compared to the older model, which itself was an impressive enough system. But, with fuel injection still a relatively early addition on motorcycles, many would find that on the 1998–9 GSX-R and even on other fuel-injected machines there would be a hesitancy low down, a hesitancy that would not be found on a well set-up, normally carburated machine.

The GSX-R750Y's big improvements were thanks to Suzuki engineer Kunio Arase, who developed the fuel injection system to work more like a traditional digital CV carburettor. Two sets of butterfly valves were controlled by the bike's new 16-bit processor 'brain'. When the rider opened the throttle and therefore the primary throttle butterfly valves, the engine management system opened the secondary set of throttle butterfly valves progressively to maintain intake velocity. The result was a complete elimination of jerky on-off throttle abruptness, as well as an increase in mid-range power.

So what did Schwantz himself have to say about the new GSX-R750Y? He recalls: 'At the launch of the 2000 GSX-R750 at Misano, I just looked at the specs of the bike and was impressed. It was something like 365lb and 140bhp – that was five or six bhp more than I had on my 1988 Daytona GSX-R, which I took pole and won the race with. Judging by these numbers, I worked out that if you took that stock bike, you should have been able to get pole that year for the race! I asked the journalists if they'd want to try and do that, they didn't offer, but there was no doubt in my mind. At the Misano 2000 launch, on Michelin tyres we were riding ten seconds off the World Superbike pole time. That's impressive.'

And so more and more accolades fell to the GSX-R750Y as the world got to taste the latest in 750 supersport machine development:

– 'Despite all the pressure from the V-twin head-banger brigade and a bevy of litre class four-banger lightweights, there hardly seems to be a more versatile or more capable streetbike-cum-racetrack tool.' *Cycle World*, July 2000.
– 'One of the sexiest production bikes yet.' *Performance Bikes*, May 2000.
– 'More power than a 750 ought to have with a mad top end rush that goes on forever.' *Bike*, July 2000.
– 'The GSX-R750 is the finest-handling Japanese sports bike this year.' *Superbike*, July 2000.
– 'GSX-R750 voted best superbike!' *Cycle World*, July 2000.
– 'Yes, thanks to the GSX-R750, the 750cc inline four is alive and well and feeling faster than ever.' *Cycle World*, July 2000.

Performance wasn't the only thing that made the GSX-R a winner. It also looked the business. *Australian Motor Cycle News* put it in a way that only the Australians can. 'The GSX-R – I was but a pup when the first Gixxer came about. I wanted one then, and I must say straight away even up against the looks of the FireBlade and R1 I'd shove this girl in my garage (its one of the few bikes that give me a chubby even with race leathers on). The other two do nothing wrong what so ever, I just fell for the Suzuki.'

Both the impressive nature of the performance of the GSX-R750Y, and the fact that in the small 750 supersport niche it was undoubted top dog, meant that the Suzuki could now take on the likes of both the sportier 600s and the 1,000cc superbikes. *Bike* magazine put the GSX-R up against the best that the supersport and litre-class could throw at it – Honda's CBR600F and Yamaha's YZF-R1. The ultimate winner was the R1, but the Suzuki was the better track bike, according to guest tester and racer Dave Redgate. 'The Suzuki really grew on me and eventually became my favourite on the track, whereas the R1 was both all-conquering and a twitchy

Warren Pole from *Two Wheels Only* magazine is a dedicated fan of GSX-Rs, running one as a long-termer while at *Superbike* magazine. (Jason Critchell)

missile, harder for a low-mileage road rider like me to get the best out of.'

In *Superbike* magazine's Sports Bike Of The Year in the October 2000 issue, the GSX-R was again up against the best from all capacity classes: the Kawasaki ZX-12R, Yamaha YZF-R1, Honda CBR900RR FireBlade, Honda VTR1000 SP-1, Aprilia RSV1000 Mille R, Ducati 748R, Kawasaki ZX-6R, and Triumph TT600. In the end the Suzuki came in fourth place, behind the R1, Mille, and FireBlade. The *Superbike* boys said: 'Overall you can't help but be impressed by a 750 that's this quick, but you can't help but be

underwhelmed by the handling, brakes and gearbox. The redesign has changed its focus, rather than improved the GSX-R's already undoubted strengths. Now it's a better all-round sportsbike and less of a race bike.'

On reflection, the 2000 GSX-R750Y did more than simply update itself again and put itself back at the top of the Superbike category. This time it had single-handedly reinvigorated the class from the doldrums of being a sparsely populated homologation racing category and made the 750 class a viable alternative to the Supersport 600 and 1,000cc class once more.

John Reynolds joined Harris Suzuki in 1996, coming off the back of a good privateer year with the Revé Kawasaki team. The bike had a stability problem at certain circuits, and his best result was a fifth place at Brno. (Mark Wernham)

The long, hard road

With an all-new bike came the fresh challenges of making it work in the showroom that is racing. The 1996 GSX-R750WT was marketed with the phrase 'built to win', which was unfortunate as it seemed the factory WSB contenders at least had something of a handling problem which would make them do anything but. But in the embryonic stages of 1996, it seemed as if things weren't too bad. The season-opening Daytona 200 race was one in which Suzuki seemed to have the trump card – Scott Russell. In early 1996 'Mr Daytona', as Russell was already known, had won three Daytona 200-milers (in later years he'd win two more and in 2001 would, sadly, suffer a career-ending injury there). He was also the factory Lucky Strike Suzuki rider in GPs, and with his laconic humour and personality was seen as a natural successor to Kevin Schwantz. Bedecked in the logos of his Lucky Strike GP team, his bike was full-factory and featured Kayaba suspension and Michelin tyres, similar to equipment used on the RGV500 GP bike.

Meanwhile the other two teams ran different set-ups. The factory Harris Suzuki squad of ex-500cc and WSB privateer John Reynolds and 1995 Aussie Superbike champ Kirk McCarthy ran Showa suspension on Michelin tyres, while the AMA Yoshimura bikes ran Öhlins suspension and Dunlops. Russell and the Lucky Strike crew had run Showas during early testing but had ditched

them for Kayabas, apparently because of familiarity.

During the run-up to the race Russell was right up there, shadowing the fast Promotor Ducati of Troy Corser, the Smokin' Joe's Honda RC45 of Miguel DuHamel, and the Muzzy Kawasaki of Anthony Gobert. The speed of the eventual poleman Corser was a thorn in Russell's side, with him complaining to journalists that the big Italian V-twins should 'be in GPs, rather than in Superbike racing against the four-cylinders.' Still, with three Daytona wins to his credit he was still fairly confident, especially in the more 'official' confines of a press conference. 'I just want to go out and win the race so Suzuki can sell lots of these motorcycles. Then I'm gonna go out and celebrate by listening to a little reggae in one of downtown Daytona's clubs…'

Reggae was the last thing on the minds of the other Suzuki runners, it seemed. The official Harris team were running with a bike that was completely built from the kit parts, but that still meant 150bhp (112KW) and 162kg (356lb). Up on the banking it seemed clear that the Harris team were having stability problems, and racing at speeds approaching 180mph (290kph) is not the time to have them. Perhaps the problem stemmed from the fact that the bike was short – 500cc GP short – based as it was on Schwantz's 1993 title-winning bike. Mat Mladin, who was riding for Yoshimura that year, admitted that perhaps the 500-style dimensions weren't

After taking Niall Mackenzie down to the wire for the 1996 *MCN* British Superbike Championship, Jamie Whitham went back to Suzuki for World Superbike duty in 1997. (Mark Wernham)

helping on the ease of set-up front, and that would account for Russell's performance on the machine, benefiting as he did from his GP crew, including experienced crew-chief Stuart Shenton. The result, in the week-delayed Daytona 200, was almost a straight-out-of-the-box victory for Suzuki. Almost. Instead, in one of the closest finishes in the race's history DuHamel on the Honda took the win by couple of inches. For anyone else on a factory Suzuki, it was a race to forget, with the Harris team returning back to the UK for testing rather than taking part in the delayed race.

In World Superbikes the writing was on the wall for Showa suspended bikes. A poor showing in the opening Misano round was a precursor of what was to come. Reynolds was 17th in the first race before crashing in the second, with McCarthy crashing in the first and coming 12th in the second race. Something needed changing and the knee-jerk reaction was suspension. At the second round at Donington Park the team had swapped to Kayaba suspension but still the problem persisted. Stability was so bad at the Hockenheim in the third round that the normally affable Reynolds refused to talk to the press and pulled out of the race, saying that he had a back injury from the Donington round. McCarthy was meanwhile feeling that perhaps the British-based team was spending a bit too much time on Reynolds rather than him as his early season form was better. Best result for the team that year was fifth in JR's hands at Brno in the Czech Republic.

At the end of the season, Reynolds reflected on the new GSX-R. 'To be honest the GSX-R is a fantastic motorcycle, it's just that due to the stability problem I'd be losing out around a quarter of a second a lap to the other guys out there and at this level of competition that's just not a problem you can afford to happen.' Team boss Lester Harris agreed: 'The handling problem only appeared at some circuits, but that

and the fact that the competition was white hot in 1996 made it bloody hard for us.'

Meanwhile over in World Endurance Terry Rymer was racing the SERT World Endurance Suzuki. In fact, Terry was riding quite a lot in 1996. Tel, always a pro-racer, was invariably good to both his sponsors and his bank manager. During 1996 he raced the Old Spice Ducati in the *MCN* British Superbike series, a Suzuki in World Endurance, and had a few cracks at GPs with the Lucky Strike GP team. To honour his commitments, Terry had to miss practice for the BSB round at Thruxton as he was still racing at Le Mans. An overnight trip in Steve Parrish's plane meant he could line up on the grid at the Hampshire track dead last on the grid. In one of the rides of the season he came through the pack to win. But what was the SERT bike like? In Gary Pinchin's book *Suzuki GSX-R750*, he said: 'When I rode the new Suzuki at the end of 1995 I felt that the engine was really good but the chassis was way off. We were running Showa at the time and couldn't get it to work so we fitted Öhlins.'

With Öhlins at the front and a Showa rear shock Rymer was on pole, but suffered chewed front tyres due to what he felt was a geometry problem. Eventually the SERT team dialled the problem out with a three-day test session at Ledenon. Rymer felt that perhaps it was the fact that the factory WSB team had little riders like Reynolds and McCarthy on board (Terry is 6ft 4in, or 2.03m). Either way, he reckoned he could get the Endurance Suzuki on to the top of the podium that year in BSB. And despite losing out in the title stakes to Kawasaki's Brian Morrison, Rymer was experienced enough to know the bike had the potential to take the title, even after the problems at Le Mans, because following the Thruxton race he told the author that: 'Pretty soon those Kawasakis won't know what hit them!' It would prove to be a prediction that would come true.

Whit at full-bore at Phillip Island in 1998. (Mark Wernham)

One man who did have a good season on the GSX-R that year was Australian Peter Goddard. Goddard – God to his fans – had shown just what a well set-up double-cradle framed GSX-R could do in 1995 with second overall in the hard-fought Australian Superbike series. In 1996 he went one better by taking the championship. His experience with the GSX-R would eventually aid development of the machine in later years, as we will see.

For the 1997 season the Harris factory Suzuki team had two new riders: Jamie Whitham, who was coming off a very successful 1996, where he'd run Niall Mackenzie so close to the *MCN*

British Superbike title; and Mike Hale, who'd had a troubled 1996 with Promotor Ducati, following a superb 1995 on the Smokin' Joe's Honda in the AMA and a couple of promising WSB rides for Promotor at the end of that year.

For Whitham, it was just what he wanted. A factory ride on the world stage. 'While on the British Superbike Yamahas, I'd got the chance to do a couple of WSB rides while Wataru Yoshikawa, the factory guy, was injured,' he said. 'I think I impressed, as I got a couple of good results and was pretty quick in qualifying and that's when Steve and Lester Harris began to talk to me about the possibility of coming back to

Suzuki. It's fair to say they'd struggled in that first year.'

The struggle for the Suzuki boys wasn't over. In the first round of the series they visited Australia's Phillip Island circuit. Here the factory World Superbike team was embarrassed by the home-grown talents and antipodean Suzukis of Troy Bayliss, the future WSB champ, who scored two fifth places, while team leader Whitham crashed out of the first race and got a 13th in the second leg. He later said: 'I could have kicked my hat around that track faster.' Things did improve during the year, with Whitham securing two podiums at the fastest tracks on the calendar. So what was the problem? Whit recalled: 'When I got on it in '97 it was a real fast bike through the speed traps. We got a couple of podiums at Monza and Hockenheim. To be honest, I think we did better than people remember. Handling was always a bit of a problem. I mean, I'm not the best at setting a bike up, but I can set one up to my liking easy enough. For my teammate Mike Hale it was a different story, as he perhaps didn't have as much experience and wasn't so good at setting it up.'

God rides for Suzuki

For 1998 things had to change. One man had shone at setting up the GSX-R over the previous few years – Pete Goddard. He was the man that the Harris brothers drafted in to develop the GSX-R into a real front runner. God bought a lot to the party. He was a double WSB winner, with wins in the early years of the series at his home rounds of Oran Park in 1989 and Phillip Island a year later. He was 1991 All-Japan champ in the years when they still raced hard-man 500cc two-

strokes, and more importantly he'd taken the Ansett Air Freight GSX-R to the Aussie Superbike title in 1996 and helped win the 1997 World Endurance championship for Suzuki. His experience made him one of the best development riders in the business – although that doesn't mean that God was thinking of spring rates rather than the win during a race!

The Aussie is blunt when describing the Harris Suzuki GSX-R: 'I came into the Harris Suzuki SBK team, a team that had the worst-handling Suzukis on earth, and I actually quickly fixed that. But compared to some of the other WSB teams we then had no engine to go with it.' Whitham recalled: 'We did a lot of work during the winter of '97 and '98. I was hardly ever at home over that winter. You'd go and test at Shah Alam or somewhere for three days but it would take another week's worth of travelling to get there and back. Tough times.'

The racing was still tough too, but despite the competition being white-hot, the Suzukis were improving. Whitham got another podium at Brands Hatch that year, while Goddard proved a much tougher teammate than Hale, getting a best of fourth at his home race at Phillip Island. By now both Whit and Goddard were regular top six finishers, mixing it with the likes of Colin Edwards and Aaron Slight on the Castrol Honda RC45, and Corser and Fogarty on the works Ducatis.

Sadly, it wasn't enough for the Harris brothers to keep hold of the contract to run the team for 1999. Instead, that would go to the Alstare set-up, which already had a major sponsor in the shape of Mexican beer giant Corona. Now the Suzuki factory would have more say over who would ride and that meant that there wasn't a place for either of the existing riders. Goddard reckoned that was a mistake. 'We didn't get the chance to continue working with the bike in 1999, although they certainly seemed to make the engine stronger. They changed teams, they

For 1999 Pier-Francesco Chili added a certain Latin colour to Suzuki's WSB efforts. (Mark Wernham)

changed everything, but had we all stayed together as a team then things would have been much stronger for Suzuki.' Whitham was also very disappointed. 'Even at the end of 1998 I felt good that I was the only one who'd ever really got any good results with the bike in World Superbike up until then, getting a few third positions.'

Instead, Pier-Francesco Chili, who had just left Ducati under a cloud, would ride alongside Japan's Katsuaki Fujiwara, who was elevated from the All-Japan Superbike championship. 'I was happy to hear that Frankie Chili would be getting a ride on the Suzuki for 1999,' explained Whitham, 'but I was a bit aggrieved

that Fujiwara was getting the other seat instead of me. I felt I'd proved enough in '98 – in fact at the end of that year I was up there battling with the likes of Slighty and Chili. I mean, I knew Fujiwara and he's a lovely guy, but I was confident I could beat him anywhere outside of Japan. Still, I'm the sort of rider who doesn't go out and pester people for rides. If they want me, they want me; if not, then I don't want to ride for some team that doesn't want me.'

The problem was that at the last race of the 1998 season at Sugo, the All-Japan Suzuki title challengers of Keichi Kitagawa and Akira Ryo were up the front and riding high, taking a one-

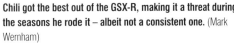

Chili got the best out of the GSX-R, making it a threat during the seasons he rode it – albeit not a consistent one. (Mark Wernham)

Frankie pops his cork at Brands Hatch in 1999. (Mark Wernham)

two in that order in race one and Ryo getting a third in race two. Enough was enough.

So, it was Francis Batta's Alstare Suzuki team that was now charged with the onerous task of turning the thus-far disappointing GSX-R into a bike capable of winning more than a race or two in the hands of the home-town Japanese riders.

It would be fair to say that with all the hard work that had gone before with the Harris team and other domestic teams, as well as Frankie being a regular winner, this was going to be the time to do the business.

Like his predecessors it took him a while to get around to business, but when he did so it was marvellous to behold. After working with Dunlop to get a tyre that would work for him both in qualifying and in the race, Frankie took pole position at round three of the 1999 championship at Donington, Suzuki's first since Doug Polen in Japan ten years earlier. A month or so later at Monza the old Frankie struck again. With a stunning home display of guile and courage he took two third position. Perhaps the GSX-R was finally coming good? It certainly seemed to be with Chili at the controls, as two rostrums later he was leading the wet Austrian round until he fell while leading by a country mile. He finally made amends and at last exorcised the factory Suzuki's ghost with a fine win in race two. At the German round in Hockenheim, he slipstreamed his way with the punchy V-twin Dukes, to slipstream Slight on the straight while outbraking Fogarty into the stadium. At the final round of the series at Sugo, Akira Ryo scored a race one win of his own.

With an overall championship position of sixth, Frankie had delivered. But after four seasons of V-twin Ducati power, what had the Suzuki been like? He said: 'My first impression was that the bike needed some changes in offset, and after some good work from the guys in my team it was not working badly. We started to get some results and we were confident.' One excellent result for the GSX-R750 in 1999 was that young Brit Karl Harris took the inaugural European Superstock title on a GSX-R750, which was impressive, as most of the bikes lined up against him were litre-class machines.

Frankie and Fujiwara were kept on board for 2000, despite the Japanese rider's lack-lustre performance and a best result of sixth all year. Encouraged by some good winter tests, and opting to use a modified version of the previous carburated bike rather than the all-new GSX-R750Y (the injected W came along in 1998, but many race teams stuck with carbs for a few years afterwards), Frankie's team expected great

things, and they got them. At last a Suzuki was in the running for the championship itself for most of the season, despite tyre problems, the odd bout of unreliability, and the GSX-R's end of season stubborn fickleness.

Although he only took one win (at Monza, where else?), Frankie took four second positions and five thirds, to come fourth in the series. Even better was the fact that Fujiwara was now beginning to come good, with improved results and a best of a third position at Misano. 'The 2000 bike was good,' said Chili. 'We improved things a little bit, and also I knew the Dunlop tyres a little more, so that worked better than the year before. The engine improved, and I was happy.'

With a good season behind him, Frankie was even happier about the prospect of an all-new bike, fuel-injected at last. 'I was waiting so much for the 2001 bike, because everyone I spoke to said it was a fantastic bike. I think the bike is very, very good on the road, but during the season we had some problems which we needed to modify but could not. So maybe we need another homologation with the frame, just to move the engine a little bit, to change the centre of gravity by putting the motor a little bit lower and further back.'

All through the 2001 season Frankie complained of the same problems: lack of corner exit grip (a must for Frankie's smooth style, where spinning the rear is bad), the bike 'running-on' into corners (with the steering unwilling to turn on a loaded front end), and the never finished task of searching for an ideal set-up which simply would not be found. He eventually finished in seventh place with a single win in the second race at Donington. His new teammate, the World Supersport champ Stephane Chambon, also struggled to come to terms with the bike, finishing the year in 12th overall. In Frankie's own words at season end: 'The problems were partly the brake and also partly acceleration, because the bike doesn't

The rise and rise of Crescent Suzuki

For years Suzuki's domestic UK presence had been non-existent. After years of gaining more publicity than they deserved through the superhuman efforts of Team Grant and Jamie Whitham, it was left to a tiny team to maintain the GSX-R's reputation in Britain.

Bournemouth-based Suzuki dealer Paul Denning had been racing the GSX-R750SPR for a couple of years backed by Crescent Suzuki, the dealership he ran with his father. In 1996 he decided to make something of the new WT and set himself up with the tall and talented Ian Cobby on the new bike. Without factory backing, but with money from his dealership and Casio G-Shock watches, he bought what kit parts he could afford and went to respected tuners TTS, based in Silverstone, and built a bike which was impressive considering their budget. Cobby had more of a pedigree in racing than Denning, but despite this both impressed in equal measure, with Denning even admitting that 'if I can't cut it on the track I will move aside for a better rider.' Eventually, Denning did take a more controlling role, and after Cobby broke a leg at the Cadwell Park round tough Scotsman Jim Moodie took to the saddle for the team, following his split from Duckhams Ducati.

Following Denning and Cobby's excellent top 15 performances and coming on the back of continual development with TTS, Moodie improved constantly, getting top ten results that showed up a number of bigger-budgeted teams. In the newly-created Production TT of that year, Sega-backed bikes in the hands of Moodie and Kiwi Shaun Harris took part in the Production 750 class. Eventually, Welshman Ian Lougher took advantage of Moodie's brake problems to take the 750 class win, while the short machine seemed to be particularly twitchy over the mountain course, where stability counts for much. Still, Moodie came second in the overall International TT Production series that year, with the same points as FireBlade-mounted winner David Jefferies, but scoring lower on countback results. 1997 saw Crescent Suzuki move up a gear – two top-notch riders in Moodie and Matt Llewellyn, more factory parts, as well as a 600 effort with the new GSX-R600. Again, the team lost out on horsepower and funding compared to the front runners, but with regular top ten performances and forays into the top five, it was only a matter of time before the factory and sponsors would sit up and take notice. In the TT, it was only the talented Marc Flynn who was doing anything worth shouting about, as the factory Hondas continued to dominate. Flynn secured fourth in the Production TT.

Paul Denning outside his shop in Bournemouth. He raced the GSX-R750SPR in 1994 and built the team up from there. Today it's the biggest in the British Superbike paddock. (Phil Masters)

For 1998, the team moved up again, recruiting old-hand Terry Rymer and young gun (though he'd been around for ages) James Haydon. With still more factory involvement and Rymer and Haydon's undoubted talent, the GSX-R was beginning to come good and come close to matching the championship-winning Yamaha YZFs of the Cadbury's Boost team. Haydon won at Silverstone and had a handful of podium placings, while Rymer also reached the podium. For 1999 Rymer left to be replaced by double Australian Superbike champ Marty Craggill. An injury meant that 'Mad Eyes' Marty couldn't replicate the form he'd shown down under, while the resurgence of the V-twins in the Superbike class meant that Haydon could do no better than his 1998 results. His defection to Red Bull Ducati left the way open for fans' favourite Chris Walker. This was the closest the GSX-R had come to a British championship since the Whitham days. Walker came straight from two seasons on the Kawasaki, where he'd been runner-up twice and runner-up the previous season on the Yamaha. Could he ever win it?

'It feels a lot smaller than my old Kawasaki and it's bloody fast too,' said Chris after initial tests on the GSX-R. One thing was for certain – he knew his way around a four-cylinder race bike better than anyone, and as the V-twin Ducatis became ever more dominant with each passing Superbike season, he was just what Suzuki needed to make the most of their machine. Just to give you an idea what spec Walker's bike was running, the whole package would have set you back a cool £85,000 (before VAT…). It was a GSX-R750 for sure, but taken to the absolute maximum. Each engine alone cost a staggering £39,000, while the forks and wheels would have left little change out of £20,000. With a ferocious amount of power and weighing less than a

Terry Rymer rode for Crescent in 1998 and took the World Endurance title for Suzuki a year later. (Double Red)

400cc road bike, this was a mad bike and a half. And in Walker, Suzuki had the perfect madman to ride it. First blood went to Walker at Albacete pre-season testing, where he went faster than any of the other title contenders, and the scene was set for the most dramatic BSB season in a long time, that saw Walker on the podium at every meeting. While his closest rival (and eventual title winner) Neil Hodgson made speed look easy on his INS Ducati 996 with a smooth and flowing style that made the most of the Duke's pinpoint steering and heady mid-range grunt, Walker looked on the verge of crashing at every corner thanks to a style so ragged it simply shouldn't work. Rarely seen with his wheels in line once off the start, Walker warmed to the Suzuki in a way he never had with a race bike before, even confessing that he'd sneak into the garage the night before the race for a quick pep talk with the machine before the next day's battle! Looking back on the season afterwards, Walker explained how he rode beyond himself on the GSX-R thanks to soaring confidence as the season went on. Part of this was down to his massive public support, part was down to the results he was notching up, but a big part was played by the bike itself, which suited his wild-sliding style to a tee.

Between BSB duties, Walker and the Suzuki found themselves on the WSB stage no less than three times in 2001 at Donington and Brands Hatch, each time notching up at least one podium finish and each time bloodying the noses of plenty of full-time factory riders. V-twins were very clearly the way to go in WSB by then,

Chris Walker was all over the place on the GSX-R, but he was the only four-cylinder challenge to Neil Hodgson's Ducati in the 2000 British Superbike championship. (Double Red)

but no one seemed to have told Walker and his Crescent GSX-R. Come the last BSB round, and Walker was leading the championship by 13 points going into the last race. All he needed was a fourth place. With the crowd behind him, he sliced up to the front of the pack, had a couple of particularly lurid slides and, for the first time all season, visibly backed off, settling for a very comfortable fourth spot and the trophy he'd always wanted. But it wasn't to be. With six laps left, entering Coppice corner, the Suzuki started to smoke, and on the following straight it was all over. The bike had dropped a valve, and all Walker could do was watch Hodgson cruise home fourth to take the title. Walker trudged back to the pits, in tears. 'As soon as someone shouted "we love you Chris," that was it, I couldn't help myself.'

Sadly, the end of 2000 saw an acrimonious parting between Walker and Suzuki. They said he had a deal to ride with them for 2001 in WSB, but he opted for GPs on the Shell Advance-backed Honda NSR500. It was sad that his dreams came to nothing half-way through the season when he was dropped from the team after a spate of crashes. Crescent soldiered on with John Crawford, who partnered Walker in 2000 and gave the team the 1998 and 1999 Supersport titles. By now the team had proliferated into the biggest team in the paddock, with representation in the Junior Superstock, Superstock, Supersport, and Superbike categories. While Crawford could not match the form of Walker in 2001, Karl Harris did take the Supersport title and now joins 2001 champ John Reynolds in the Crescent line-up for the 2002 campaign on GSX-R1000s.

Walker's season was all smiles to begin with, then tears as his bike dropped a valve in the last round when he had one hand on the championship, and finally acrimony when he moved to Honda in 500cc GPs. (Double Red)

have enough grip from the rear, especially if you have too much weight in the front. Maybe Suzuki don't have a programme to improve in this direction.'

It was sad that at the end of 2001 Frankie was disillusioned with the Suzuki. 'All year we had the same problem and we finished the year with the same bike. It was not so good, and I don't like to continue like that or to work in this way. So I said to my team, "I quit." But I still like the Francis Batta team because I think it is the best team in Superbike.' Even a season end war of words and recrimination did not sour Chili's feelings about his old team, even if some outsiders pointed fingers at them, giving the example of the success enjoyed by Akira Ryo winning the All-Japan series that year, or Mat Mladin in the USA winning his third AMA title on the trot with similar bikes. Frankie remains unconvinced about racers doing well on the GSX-R750 in what he sees as lesser championships. 'You can see the answer yourself,' he explains, 'because you see when we go in America we have the World Superbike race one day later than the "local" race, and even though I could not do all the WSB race, we saw that Eric Bostrom [top finishing local AMA man in SBK, on another four-cylinder bike, the Kawasaki] makes two fifth places, I think, and he never won the American championship. When Mat was in the race, he lost compared to the other American guys and he was on a Suzuki. It is the same problem in Japan. I did not see Ryo get so far away from me at Sugo even if it is his home track. It is not an excuse. Local riders normally go very well at their home tracks. Look at Izutsu on the Kawasaki – he makes some good races in Japan, but we never see him on so high a level in Europe.'

Possibly the most frustrating part of the whole GSX-R 2001 experience for Frankie was that, as Haga had demonstrated in 2000, the right 750 four-cylinder could win races, and challenge for the championship. 'Sure you can have some more from the bike. If I can use the bike in the same system in the corner sure, I have more speed on the straight, and therefore I could improve on my lap time. Sure it could be improved from last year.'

Chili's GSX-R Championship ambitions may have ended in frustration, but he was easily the most successful GSX-R exponent in the 14 year history of World Superbike racing. For 2002 the burden of carrying the GSX-R flag will fall again to the Alstare team, despite a mid-season question mark over Suzuki's involvement. In a smaller, one-man team, Spaniard Gregorio Lavilla will ride the 2002 GSX-R750, while in a two-man effort Chambon will return to the class he was champ in, alongside Fujiwara.

As if heeding Chili's parting words, the chassis of the 2002 machine will feature a host of changes. The new bike has a different swingarm pivot point and revised steering head angle. Changing the swingarm pivot mount – which will be featured on the 2002 road-going GSX-R750s for homologation purposes – will allow a greater range of adjustability of the rear suspension. Making the steering head angle steeper will allow the bike to turn-in quicker. Another advantage is that the Suzuki, like all four-cylinder machines in WSB, can now weigh in at 159kg (350lb) compared to twins at 164kg (361lb). Perhaps with rule changes and the odd tweak here and there, one day soon the World Superbike title – a title Suzuki have worked hard for and want so badly – will finally go to a GSX-R. With the prospect of rule changes to lower the perceived twin-cylinder machine advantages, whether it will be with a GSX-R750 or a GSX-R1000 remains to be seen.

Mat Mladin: triple treat

Mat Mladin was marked out for greatness early on, failed to fulfil that promise, and then did so, pretty much in that order. The 1992 Australian Superbike champion was snapped up by Cagiva to ride their fast-improving GP 500 alongside Doug Chandler, but failed to impress and was replaced by John Kocinski. Mladin is a tough cookie and decided to go back to the drawing board. When he appeared in the USA riding for Yoshimura in 1996, Mladin was starting to impress as much as he had four years previously, with a fourth place overall in the AMA series on the new 750WT. He went one better in 1997 with the Fast by Ferracci Ducati

squad, challenging eventual winner Doug Chandler for most of the year, but moved back to Yoshimura for 1998. Again he was the nearly man, winning the last race of the season, but not the title, as winless Chandler and Honda's Ben Bostrom decided that, with Chandler losing the title through an oil leak. By 1999 Mladin, the team, and the bike knew each other intimately, and despite losing out to DuHamel in the Daytona 200 he went on to take the title.

For 2000, the team – as in WSB – stuck to the previous bike, which didn't matter as Mladin still won. For 2001 he had the new machine, the sort of factory support that hadn't been seen since Schwantz's time with the team, and a return from Mat's old Kawasaki days, crew chief Peter Doyle. Doyle brought many of the top antipodeans into World Superbikes through the late 1980s and early 1990s. With the team concentrating on improving the feedback and grip from the front-end of the bike, Mladin opened his 2001 account with his second successive Daytona victory, before telling his rivals: 'I want to win this championship and will do everything I can to win it and another and another.' It wasn't plain sailing. His foes included Eric Bostrom on the Kawasaki, Nicky Hayden on the Honda VTR (RC51 in the States), who won the last four races of the season, and even Mladin's countryman Anthony Gobert, who took Yamaha to its first AMA Superbike race win since 1994. Gobert looked like a contender until breaking his arm and concentrating on the 600 series thereafter.

Mladin had his injuries too. A moto cross crash at home in Australia meant he had to come back from a broken left lower leg, but the points cushion he'd built up early on meant that, despite young Hayden's last-gasp rush, the title was his, regardless of his uncharacteristic distant 12th in the final round. Still, that was the way to win it, to do just enough. Schwantz, team adviser to Yoshimura, summed it up: 'He's got such a good head on his shoulders. He thinks "Championship, championship, championship", 100 per cent of the time at the racetrack and probably 100 per cent of the time away from the racetrack. He's got a great bunch of guys around him. It seems like they're always a step ahead.'

It was only the third time a rider had won three titles in a row and the first time it had been done on a Suzuki. One last piece of the Mladin puzzle remains to fit into place – the world stage. Is he the one to take the GSX-R to the Holy Grail of the World Superbike championship?

Mat Mladin (number 66) at the start of the 1999 Daytona 200. He would come second, but would win the championship that year, and the next, and the next! (Suzuki)

The new-for-2001 GSX-R600 again aped its bigger brothers. Here's *Two Wheels Only* magazine's Gus Scott 'getting it reet over'. (Jason Critchell)

It's a family affair

It was inevitable that such a successful machine as the GSX-R750 should spawn a family of different capacity machines all bearing that legendary moniker. But it was a smaller capacity machine that actually bore the GSX-R name first, a whole year before the 750 hit the streets.

In Japan the smaller 250cc two-stroke and 400cc four-stroke capacities have long been important as tough machine, and license laws make it easier to ride and buy these smaller machines than the larger bikes popular in Europe in the mid to late 1980s. In 1984 the first in a long line of GSX-Rs was released – in Japan, naturally.

Ironically the GSX-R400 didn't look as dated as its year younger 750 brother. There was no double-cradle frame or twin headlights. Instead there was a single light and a much more modern-looking aluminium beam frame, that wrapped itself around the diddy four-cylinder motor which redlined at 13,000rpm. As the years went on and the familiar shape of the GSX-R750 became accepted as the iconic sports machine it was, the GSX-R400 – in a further twist of irony – switched to a smaller copy of the trademark double-cradle frame for the 1990 GSX-R400RRL. This machine was a real mini GSX-R, with 60bhp and a redline of 14,500rpm. Basically, the variants of the GSX-R400 followed the same designations as the bigger 750 as the years rolled on, even including a trick RR-SP version with fully adjustable suspension and close-ratio

gearbox for Sports Production racing. The machine would continue to do well in Japan, but in the UK it was left to 'Grey Importers' to bring the machine to the notice of the bike-buying British public. (Grey bikes were machines that, during the mid to late 1990s, took advantage both of favourable pound to yen conversion rates and the reluctance of UK importers to bring these pocket marvels into the country.)

The GSX-R400RR would make usable power from around 8,000rpm before hitting its maximum of around 55bhp at 11,200rpm. It was gorgeous, it was manic, and it handled, and there was something about pinging the little four-cylinder cylinder motor up to its 14,000rpm redline. It even had the GSX-R name. And yet still it wasn't the most popular Grey sports 400 of the time – Honda's VFR400 and CBR400RR saw to that. The 400 wasn't to be the smallest capacity machine to carry the GSX-R name, as Suzuki produced a 250cc inline four, mainly for the Japanese market, at the end of the 1980s. Again, it had a beam frame rather than the signature double-cradle and again it was only found in the UK courtesy of Grey importers.

Okay, so these little urchins didn't have three figure power outputs, but there was something about revving the nuts off the bike and *still* being a GSX-R that mattered to many buyers. The 400's full-on race image was further helped in Japan by top racer Doug Polen winning F3 championships on it. In Gary Pinchin's excellent

It took a real man to do this… The GSX-R1100G in full flight.
(Suzuki)

book *Suzuki GSX-R750*, Polen says: 'It was a gas to ride. I mean that thing was cool. 250 slicks. Rail city. I was riding two different bikes, one – the 400 – was like riding a 250GP machine and then I had to get on the superbike on the same day. Like it was grip city with the smaller bike and then I'd have to battle with the superbike – I was more than happy to get on the 400 – any time!' I lis delight with the smaller GSX-R resulted in five wins from eight races and the F3 title in 1989. The future would hold World Superbike, AMA and World Endurance glory for Polen.

The mother of all GSX-Rs, in size if not age, came on the scene two years after the 400 and a year after the launch of the seminal 750. This was Suzuki's GSX-R1100G of 1986. It was similar in shape and style to the 750 of that year, but as the

world headed towards the 'greed-is-good' philosophy of the late 1980s the 1100 seemed to take all this to heart.

In a similar way to its revolutionising of the 750 class, Suzuki looked at the big litre bikes of the time and decided to give the class the GSX-R treatment. To start with Suzuki gave the 1100G a claimed 130bhp and a 197kg (433.4lb) dry weight. Compared to the competition it was in a different league. It was lighter than the Kawasaki GPZ1000RX by 43kg (94.6lb) and posted high ten second quarter-mile standing start times. And it would take most manufacturers the best part of ten years to beat with their production bikes. At its heart was a 1,052cc motor which was 14kg (30lb) lighter than the legendary GSX1100 engine, as well as being 72mm (2.8in) narrower.

The silhouette was the same as the 750, but the power was way, way up. (Suzuki)

As on the 750, SACS (Suzuki Advanced Cooling System) was used, as well as the new TSCC (Twin Swirl Combustion Chamber) and similar, but at 34mm much bigger, flat-slide carbs.

Suzuki claimed that the 1100 had the best power to weight ratio of the time – 1.51kg (3.3lb) per brake horse power. The chassis also aped its little brother, following the characteristic double-cradle curves, being made of aerospace quality aluminium, and weighing in at just 12.8kg (28lb). Brakes at the front were two 310mm floating discs with four-piston opposed calipers. Weight distribution was also the ideal figure of the time of 50 per cent over each wheel, although the sheer size of the beast as well as a comparatively tiny wheelbase of 1,460mm (56.9in) meant that a steering-damper was *de rigeur*.

Out on the road or on the track, this was an awesome machine producing good power from low down in the rev range, but with the motor really coming into life at around 5,000rpm. Mat Oxley got his first taste of the awesome power of the big Suzuki at its launch at the Laguna Seca and he simply said: 'I'm convinced that the GSX-R1100 is the best sports superbike ever.' In their own way the UK's *Superbike* magazine agreed, saying: 'It's a trouser-filler if ever there was one!' Later in high-speed testing around Millbrook's banked track, the magazine could see the bike was a handful at speed. 'I knew it was shifting around,' the tester said at the time, 'that much was obvious to me clinging on the top – but I hadn't realised the effect of the banking on the handling until I stopped by the photographer and

By the time the final models of the 1100 came out it was
losing out to its competitors. Despite this, veterans like Grant
Leonard could still have some fun. (Superbike)

looked at his face. He admitted to getting a shot
and then ducking behind the Armco because he
was convinced a massive accident was about
to happen!'

According to journalists, against its
competition of the time the Suzuki was a
winner in all but touring ability, as the big GSX-
R's uncompromising attitude made it a harsher
prospect over long distances. It proved to be a
winner in the showrooms, too, being updated
in 1987 with the H-model, coming also as a
limited edition in black and gold 'Hyper-
Endurance' paint scheme. For 1988 Suzuki
gave the 1100J a wider rear tyre, now a 160
rear section, but it was the 1989 model that
would give the entire GSX-R1100 range a bad
name. With the competition getting hotter with
the likes of the Kawasaki ZX-10 and the
Yamaha FZR1000 Genesis coming on the

scene, Suzuki were under pressure to give the
big bruiser a real shot in the arm.

Again the bigger machine aped its little brother
of the time and seemed to follow the successful
relaunch of the GSX-R750. The 1989 GSX-
R1100K featured the legendary 'Slingshot' name
across its flanks and a host of changes
underneath, which included a 25 per cent stiffer
frame than before, a wheelbase that had shrunk
from 1,460mm to 1,425mm (56.1in), and
matching that finally with 17-inch wheels. While
the chassis dimensions had shrunk, save for an
increase in dry weight to 210kg (462lb), the
motor grew. Now it was a whopping 1,127cc
from the original 1,052cc, with a higher 10:1
compression ratio and with bigger 36mm Mikuni
carbs rather than the original 34mm CV ones,
and with a claimed 143bhp. This mighty
leviathan was launched at Circuito de Jerez in

...But you could still have fun on it, as demonstrated by Martin 'Wild' Child. (*Bike* magazine)

southern Spain and many journalists came away with very positive views. Grant Leonard of *Superbike* magazine was gushing in his praise. 'It's like a caged animal on the twisty switchback circuit. But it's a forgiving bike. Feels rock solid and controllable when cranked over.'

Then something bizarre happened. For some strange reason the big Suzuki changed between the press launch and the production line. This mild-mannered soppy beast suddenly became a raging animal. Many felt that Suzuki had altered the weight distribution to put more weight over the front of the machine which simply ruined its handling. Either way, something had happened between launch and production, as Leonard explained: 'We were expecting the 1100 Slingshot to be something really special as the 750 was a belter. We weren't disappointed, the 1100 was a wheelie monster. You could pick it up

on the power in second so easily. But, when we got the bikes back in the UK, people were riding the things through hedges and doing daft things with them. We don't know what Suzuki did to them, but they were different. Perhaps our talk of "easy to wheelie" meant that the Japanese pushed weight over the front or something. Journalists on launches should always remember the bikes they ride are pre-production! I even got to ride the Whitham and Mellor race bikes from that year and they felt similar, although obviously a lot better sorted.'

Sadly this is something that Suzuki seems to be noted for. At the time of the launch of the two-stroke RG500, journalists were impressed with a power output that was over 100bhp at least, but then when the machines finally came to the UK they were struggling to hit 90. It was the same with the V-twin TL1000S, which many agreed

handled better on the launch than back home – pock-marked roads or no. Similarly to the RG500, Suzuki's GSX1300R Hayabusa also seemed to be a little bit more frisky in the engine department on launch than when coming from the main importer. It's understandable to see why a company would do such a thing. If the journalists tell potential buyers the bike is a rocket ship which handles perfectly, it's going to sell … but if the bike isn't the same as the one which the punter buys, then what's the point? Still, fiddling with test and launch bikes has happened in the bike world for years, ranging from just a 'good service' to an interesting five per cent hike over the quoted power figures.

A year later, perhaps in a bid to calm the bike down a little, the 1100L featured a longer swingarm which took the wheelbase out to 1,465mm (57.7in), a less extreme head angle of 25.2°, and multi-adjustable upside-down front forks and rear shock. For the first time the 1100 used a wider 180-section rear tyre. While things altered a little, the whole weight distribution issue was never addressed and the GSX-R1100 was getting a reputation as a 143-claimed-bhp beast. A reputation not helped by the death of the well-liked Phil Mellor in the 1989 1300 Production TT on a GSX-R1100. Irrespective of blame (and to be fair, Mez's team-boss and fellow legend Mick Grant never blamed the bike's handling or tyres for the crash), the fact was that this tragedy was part of a bigger one for the Production race that year and effectively killed top-line production racing at the TT for the next seven years, as well as on the UK mainland.

But still the 1100 wobbled on. Sometimes quite literally. The 1100M featured a new aerodynamic package which included the familiar twin-beam headlights now hidden beneath a clear fairing, bigger 40mm CV carbs which traded a monster top-end power boost for a dip in mid-range grunt, revised cylinder head, and a 25.83° steering head angle. The result was a 149bhp

machine which weighed in at 226kg (498lb). The beast was getting heavier and being left behind by the likes of the Yamaha FZR1000 EXUP. A garish graphic change for the 1100N of 1992 didn't help. By now the Kawasaki ZZ-R1100 was the undisputed speed king, the EXUP ruled the roost, and the new CBR900RR FireBlade was making its presence felt. Something had to be done.

What was eventually done had been done on the GSX-R750 a year earlier. Yet again the 750 blazed a trail which its bigger brother had to wait a year for: liquid-cooling. The 1993 GSX-R1100WP was heralded as the most powerful production bike ever when it finally hit the streets. Suzuki claimed a massive 151bhp (112.6kW), which was good for at least 130bhp (96kW) at the rear tyre. All this power came from a smaller capacity (1,074cc) and a raised compression ratio of 11.2:1. In the chassis department Suzuki stiffened up the frame, lengthened the wheelbase to 1,485mm (58.5in), lowered the centre of gravity by dropping the motor an inch lower in the frame, and gave the bike a steering head angle of 24.5°.

Despite all this extra oomph in the engine room, this liquid-cooled version had perhaps less mid-range than the older motors and it still had to haul 231kg (508.2lb) of machinery around. Still, the GSX-R11 remained a performer, with the UK's *Performance Bikes* magazine getting 134.8bhp (100.6kW) at 9,750rpm from their bike, which propelled it to a 174mph (280kph) top speed and a 10.5 second standing-start quarter mile time. The 1994 version, the WR, featured a new paint job only.

The final version of the much-loved GSX-R1100, the WS, came along in 1995. Here at last Suzuki set about cutting weight from the big machine and giving it back a bit of mid-range. They started by cutting 10kg (20.2lb) off the dry weight as well as adding a new swingarm and much better suspension. In the motor you had new cams, different valve timing, revised ignition, and also a new twin-exit exhaust (only one end can was actually needed; the other was for noise emissions). Add to that sharper looks courtesy of 750-lookalike multi-reflector headlights and a much more comfortable riding position, and the GSX-R1100 seemed to be back on track.

'Like any GSX-R, the engine is the heart of the beast,' explained John Cantlie of *Superbike* when he first rode the WS. 'The new cams and ignition have given the GSX-R1100 the sort of mid-range that a litre monster should have. Gone is that evil, irritating flat-spot at 5,000rpm, instead it's replaced by a great, hairy lunge of power that launches bike and rider into escape velocity.' Handling was also praised by Sonic. 'With the 1995 GSX-R real A-road mashing is possible, thanks to the revised frame and suspension. The new riding position is dead spiffy, easily as comfortable as a ZZ-R1100 and your legs aren't curled up behind your bum like on the old bike, so the rider can chuck the bike around like a good 'un!'

The 1995 GSX-R proved to be one of the best of the long-line of 1,100cc machines produced during that nine-year period. Sadly, by the time the much improved WS appeared in 1995 the market had moved on. The last 1100 model imported into the UK was 1996's 1100WT, before being discontinued in November of that year. Ironically, the bike which had done so much to revolutionise big-bore sportsbikes had been left behind by the likes of the Honda CBR900RR FireBlade and others.

Still, there was life in the old girl yet, with many 1100s attempting to become the fastest tuned production bikes in the world, or becoming stunt bikes, streetfighters, and 7/11s (of which more in the owning chapter). In fact, it would be fair to say that just as much of the cult of the GSX-R name is down to the 1100 as the 750, so while many bemoaned the loss of the butchest of all the mighty Gixxers when it was suddenly struck from the dealers' showrooms at the end of 1996, then just remember this. In his report on the GSX-R1100WS, *Superbike*'s John Cantlie opined that if the 1100 continued its diet, then within four years Suzuki would produce a machine with 153bhp (114KW) at the rear wheel and a weight of just 180kg (396lb). He may have been a bit out with the capacity and the year of entry, but just after the turn of the century a remarkable GSX-R would come along with that sort of spec. More of which later…

The GSX-R600: Supersport treat

Ironically, in the same year that the first GSX-R750 was launched, a machine came on to the scene which re-invigorated the middleweight sportsbike class: the Kawasaki GPZ600R.

Since the GPZ of 1985, over the next decade and a half the supersport 600 class had become perhaps the most important sports machine class in the world. And yet during the late 1980s and early 1990s, Suzuki had nothing with which to really take the fight to the opposition in Europe. They had the GSX600F – known as the 'Katana' in the USA, after its more illustrious forbears from the 1980s (and 'The Teapot' in the UK, thanks to its slightly curious fully-enclosed bodywork styling!) – a good bike, featuring a solid enough engine which would later come

The GSX-R600 was a miniature of the 750WT – especially if it was in the corporate blue and white. (Suzuki UK)

back to life in the popular GSF Bandit 600 range, and a steel box-section frame. But it was never the sportiest of the 600s available. Despite this, it was campaigned out on track by the indomitable Jamie Whitham, although paddock legend allegedly has it that he and mentor Mick Grant were running the bike at nearer 750cc. Still, as sporty bikes were what was selling at the time in the UK, Suzuki deleted the GSX from its range in the mid-1990s.

In 1993 Suzuki tried a different tack, producing the RF600. This machine was more in line with a sports tourer than a sports machine, and despite being a good enough bike it disappeared without a trace at the end of 1996, ironically just

about the same time as the trusty old GSX Teapot was being reintroduced into the UK.

Despite having two bikes with the right capacity, Suzuki knew they needed something a bit more special and sporty to make a killing in this popular class. A GSX-R600 had been around in the USA for a few years from 1992, but all it comprised was a GSX-R750 chassis with a sleeved-down engine, which while it looked the part wasn't the ideal solution. Eventually the solution came. In 1997 Suzuki launched its all-new GSX-R600V at Homestead Raceway in Florida. It looked almost identical to the updated, beam-framed 750 introduced the previous year, save for a set of conventional rather than upside-

...Or in this lovely yellow. (Suzuki UK)

down front forks. This wasn't surprising, as the 600 project was actually started at the same time as the 1996 GSX-R750T, but was held back a year for the bigger bike to make an impression and establish itself. Despite the claims that this machine was a complete 'clean sheet of paper' project, the two models shared the same mainframe, although with a 10mm shorter swingarm. All told the chassis was 1.5 kg (3.3lb) lighter than the 750. The engine, too was lighter, by 3.5kg (7.7lb), utilising ignition coils built into the sparkplug caps, which saved almost half a kilo. Whatever Suzuki said, ostensibly the 600 was a carbon-copy of the 750 but with smaller holes in the motor, 10mm less wheelbase, and all

for a fair bit less moolah. It was the lightest machine in its class at just 195kg (429lb), had chunky 45mm forks, a 180 rear-section tyre, and a claimed 100bhp (74kW).

It impressed from the word go. Olly Duke of *Bike* magazine said: 'If any machine could be accused of having an attitude problem in the 600 class this is the one. Not much happens below 5,000rpm, it only starts to pick up at 7,000rpm and it doesn't seriously come into life until you hit 10,000rpm. It begs to be thrashed and abused. When you're in tune with keeping it on the boil it's tops, but when you're not in the mood it's a pain. When you're getting fed-up of the GSX-R's peaky performance you're also starting to feel

And the latest version even comes in this Movistar Suzuki replica of the Suzuki GP squad. (Suzuki UK)

horribly cramped, but come those summer trackdays and no other 600 will be able to corner as quick.'

John Cantlie from *Superbike* was in agreement. This 600 was a racetrack refugee. 'I was having to slip the clutch like a two-stroke on one tortuously tight left hander. At 6,000rpm there's not much to play with on the GSX-R. Above 10,000rpm and she takes off. Nice typical Suzuki screaming power all the way to 13,500rpm and beyond.'

The Suzuki was a big hit, providing the sportiest thrills in the class, compared to its rivals. The handling and brakes were universally praised, although criticism still came in the form of just *how* the power came in. This criticism was easily cured in the form of stage one tuning with the removal of the very restrictive end-can with a

top-quality one such as Yoshimura or Micron, re-jetting, and fitting a freer-flowing air filter. Results of nine per cent more power and torque were common, as well as getting rid of that hole between 5 and 6,000 revs. To try and address the lack of mid-range as standard the 1998 GSX-R600W featured updates to the motor to give the machine a little more mid-range stomp.

But if the machine was criticised for being *too* sporty then the answer came from the original GSX-R600's project leader Kunio Arase, who told journalists at the launch: 'The new GSX-R600 is simply designed to win Supersport 600 races.' And win it did. In the UK Scotsman John Crawford took a brace of championship wins in the hard-fought Supersport 600 series in 1998 and 1999, with the machine even taking overall world Supersport 600 honours in the hands of

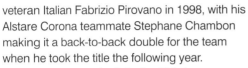

The race 600 had rather good brakes, according to Karl Harris, who took the bike to victory in the 2001 British Supersport series. (Gold and Goose)

veteran Italian Fabrizio Pirovano in 1998, with his Alstare Corona teammate Stephane Chambon making it a back-to-back double for the team when he took the title the following year.

Pretty soon standards in the 600 class were moving faster than in any other sports category and by 1999 the GSX-R600 was looking a little past it compared to the latest Honda CBR600F, Kawasaki ZX-6F, and especially the overtly sporty Yamaha YZF-R6. So, as the GSX-R750Y came about in 2000, so did a doppelganger 600, in the form of the 2001 GSX-R600.

The new clothes, like the previous GSX-Rs, mimicked the bigger bike, but again under the surface it was much-changed. The engine for the latest 600 was a whole 4kg (8.8lb) lighter than the previous model's, thanks to a smaller cylinder head which was 900gm (2lb) lighter, smaller valve stems which saved 48gm (1.7oz), and alloy valve springs which saved a further 192gm (6.8oz). The completed motor was also 9.5mm shorter and 6mm lower in height than the previous version. To get a claimed 115bhp (85.8kW) from it, the compression ratio was raised to 12.1–12.2:1 and the airbox was increased by 1.3l to 11.3l capacity. Straighter, shorter intake ports improved the mixture's route into the combustion chamber as well as more efficient combustion 'bang' when it got there.

Just as the 2000 GSX-R750Y utilised fuel injection so did the new 600. The injectors on this system were angled at 60° to the intake valves for an optimal spray of fuel/air mix to the individual combustion chambers. To help get the optimum amount of air into the engine for any given throttle position, Suzuki used its dual throttle valve system (SDTV) which had two valves per throttle body, so that one was connected to the twist-grip itself and the other was servo-controlled, which would open and close progressively in line with the first to maintain maximum intake speed. This would help give the fuel injection system a much

smoother, linear feel than the jerkiness of earlier FI systems. Chassis-wise, the wheelbase was cut by 15mm to 1,385mm (54.5in), but it shared the steering geometry figures of the previous model of 24° of rake and 96mm (3.8in) of trail. Weight distribution went from 50/50 front and back to a more nose-heavy 51.4 per cent over the front

wheel. Overall weight was down to just 163kg (358.6lb) thanks to reductions in the weight of the Tokico brake calipers and Pirelli making a special lightweight tyre.

Like the introduction of the original 600 three years before, the new fuel-injected GSX-R600 wasn't the quantum leap the original GSX-R750 was over the opposition, but it showed just what years of refinement could do. Warren Pole from *Superbike* magazine rated it highly. 'The styling's hard as nails, the motor is a silky screamer and the handling really is superb. Throw in strong brakes, useful stuff like a protective screen, a U-lock space under the

seat and a clock and this is a mighty impressive motorcycle.'

Again, in the UK the bike was a success on road and track. *Two Wheels Only* magazine not only said it was the best 600cc Supersport machine of the year, but also put it in its Top Five bikes of the year, claiming it was 'one of the finest GSX-Rs ever.' Out on the track the machine was up at the front in the World Supersport 600 championship. It won the Australian Supersport championship with youngster Josh Brookes on board, and in the UK Karl Harris took the 2001 British Supersport 600 title on it. Not bad for the updated machine's debut year.

Suzuki's GSX-R1000: the ultimate supersport machine

With the striking of the 1100 from dealers' showrooms at the end of 1996, and considering the UK and Europe's love of big-bore sportsbikes such as the FireBlade, ZX-9R, and R1, it made sense that Suzuki, too, would build a pared-to-the-bone big-bore supersports machine. Thankfully they did, and the end result was the GSX-R1000, which was launched at the end of 2000 ready for the 2001 model year.

Understandably, Suzuki based this machine on the smaller 750, which was almost proving a match to the bigger class of machines such as the Yamaha YZF-R1 and Honda CBR900RR FireBlade. The GSX-R1000 chassis was nigh-on identical to the GSX-R750Y, except that it was just 4kg (8.8lb) heavier and ran Kayaba instead of Showa suspension. At the rear was a Kayaba piggy-back shock which was 180gm (6.3oz) lighter and had a 35 per cent reduction in 'stiction' (a sticky form of friction which stops objects moving smoothly against one another)

over the 750's shocker. The front forks themselves looked stunning as they benefited from being nitrided. This is a shimmering coating which cuts down on stiction. The forks were 360gm (12.7oz) lighter than those of the 750 and 5mm shorter. Also at the front were new six-pot calipers which were 15 per cent more rigid and 15 per cent lighter than their previous incarnation. The rear brake was also 60gm (2.1oz) lighter than that on earlier GSX-Rs.

The frame joined to the engine in two places rather than one and featured frame walls that were 0.5mm thicker than on the 750. This, along with a stiffer swingarm, made the whole chassis seven per cent more rigid than the 750. Tyre-wise you had an enormous 190 rear-section, while the front Bridgestone 011 was unique in having a softer sidewall design to improve mid-corner grip. The 988cc motor utilised a fuel injection system similar to that of the latest 750 and 600 machines, but with one important addition – the

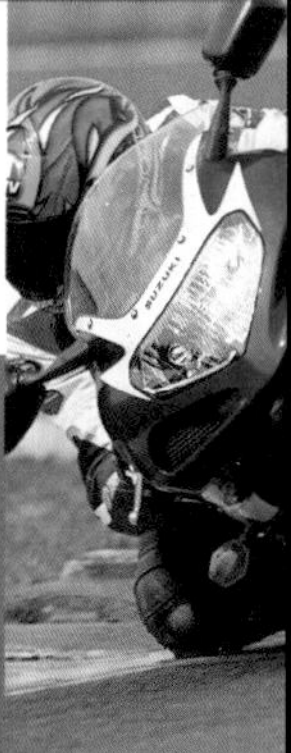

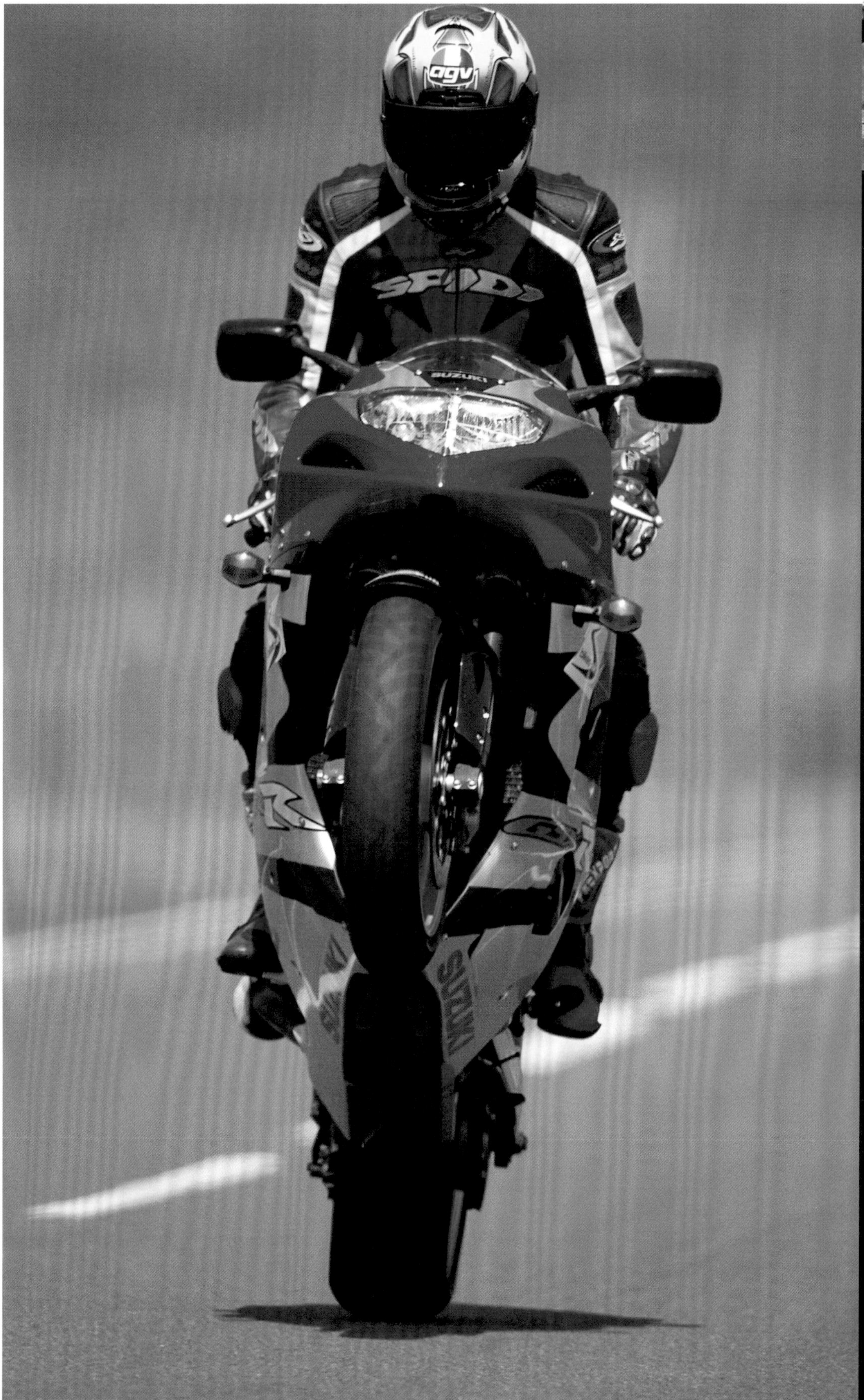
agv
SPIDI
SUZUKI
SUZUKI

The new Crescent GSX-R1000 racer … 180 'claimed' bhp.
(John Noble)

Suzuki Exhaust Tuning system, or SET for short. This is similar to the old Yamaha EXUP valve, found on many Yams since the late '80s and, since the ending of the 10 year patent on its design, imitated on many other bikes, including Honda's Y2K FireBlade and the 2001 GSX-R1000.

Building exhaust systems is always a compromise based on where you want your power: in the low and mid-range, or up the top end of the rev-range. The way these powervalves work is that a butterfly valve opens and shuts at the right time to fool the engine into thinking it has different length header pipes, and different back pressures, which means you can liberate the benefits of more low-down 'oomph' as well as having that top-end hit. The SET system is a little more complex than early powervalves, taking readings of engine rpm, gear selection, and throttle position before opening and closing the valve in the collector pipe accordingly. In

addition, the GSX-R1000 had an extra dollop of memory in its fuel injection CPU (up from 8-bit and 32k of ROM on the 750 to 16-bit and 96K of ROM on the 1000), and bigger 42mm throttle bodies. Pistons on the 1000 were actually 3gm *lighter*, despite being 1mm larger in bore.

Overall, this beast weighed in at just 170kg (374.4lb) and pumped out an astonishing 161 claimed brake horsepower at 11,000rpm. While many GSX-R fans would have loved to see the 1100 badge come back to life, improvements in engine design now meant that more than enough power could be obtained from just one litre. Even very experienced motorcyclists were astonished at just how close the GSX-R1000 was to a four-stroke race machine. Shades of the original GSX-R750?

Launched at Road Atlanta in Florida, it was soon evident that the 1000 was going to replace the Yamaha YZF-R1 as the king of the sports machines. *Superbike* sent then editor John Cantlie to the launch. He said: 'The GSX-R1000 is

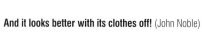

And it looks better with its clothes off! (John Noble)

plainly built to compete with the R1 and FireBlade. It's based very heavily on the company's existing 750 – cylinder head, wheelbase, steering angles and fuel injection system are all the same. In essence it's a bored and stroked 750 to arrive at its 988cc final capacity – but does it work? Well, put it this way, I've never witnessed a bunch of motorcycle journalists reduced so quickly to a gaggle of babbling school kids. The Suzuki GSX-R1000 rips – plain and simple. I reckon the newest kid on the block won't just beat the opposition, it'll kick them all over the shop.'

Niall Mackenzie, a triple British Superbike champion and seven-time podium finisher in 500cc GPs, had retired and found himself a job on a new motorcycle magazine called *Two Wheels Only.* His first job? Riding the GSX-R1000 around Jerez circuit against a number of other sports machines. He couldn't believe it. 'I spend a lot of my time testing GSX-R750 superbikes which cost £80,000 and yet this GSX-R1000

offers around 80 per cent of the performance for about a tenth of the cost!'

Everywhere the GSX-R was sold the story was the same. The R1 and FireBlade were defeated as the very ultimate in the sportsbike class. It picked up *MCN*'s Machine of the Year as well as the overall International Bike of the Year, which is awarded annually after votes from many magazines world-wide. It then picked up the '*Superbike* Bike of the Year' title in that magazine's annual shoot-out with its peers in the October 2001 issue, as well as the *Performance Bikes* 'Sportsbike of the Year' title during the same month.

Superbike editor Kenny Pryde said: 'The Suzuki GSX-R1000 is Superbike of the Year by miles. From the first couple of laps the others were only fighting for second … This is a truly spectacular motorcycle.' Trevor Franklin, road test editor for *Performance Bikes*, agreed: 'Suzuki has pulled off a major coup by beating their rivals at their own game. More power, better

Niall Mackenzie got to try it out at the GSX-R Festival. (Author)

suspension and handling to shame the lot of them.' To illustrate the depth of class the GSX-R family possessed by now, *Superbike* magazine placed the GSX-R600 in second place and the 750 in fifth, while PB placed the 750 third and the 600 sixth.

Even in its inaugural year of racing, the big Suzuki ruled the roost. In the hands of Paul Young it took the British Superstock title, in a season where the majority of the top 15 had them. It would take nine wins from the 11 races held that year. In World Endurance in 2001, seven of the eight rounds in the Super Production class were won by the GSX-R1000, and with rule changes moving towards the

bigger machines, who's to say the Suzuki won't be favourite for overall honours in 2002? The 1000 also took the World Superstock title in the hands of young British rider James Ellison and the Australian Superbike championship – by this time allowing big four-cylinder machines on the grid – in the hands of Shawn Giles, his second successive title, having won previously on a GSX-R750. In the USA, Suzuki scored its first ever AMA Formula Extreme Championship with 18-year-old John Hopkins, who will start 2002 in GPs with Red Bull Yamaha. In the All-Japan series, Keiichi Kitigawa won the production based Super Naked class with seven wins and two second places out of nine starts.

With four-stroke rule changes in the UK changing towards the big 1,000cc fours, and with World Superbike rules surely not far behind, perhaps the days of GSX-R domination in classes other than superstock are just around the corner. Not surprising, then, that the bike's marketing campaign was 'Own the Racetrack'. It certainly did!

In a bid to get the jump on the opposition, in early 2001 Cresecent Suzuki began building a GSX-R1000 which was their interpretation of the up-coming rules. Boss Paul Denning said: 'It made sense to start building something as soon as possible to fit in with the new rules. For us, we wanted to see which direction in which to go – 750 Superbike or the 1,000cc machine. We had to get the thing up and running as soon as possible to gauge just how well it would work.' After a swift gestation period, the bike was built, featuring all the chassis luxuries you'd see on a Superbike with the sort of power you'd find on a Grand Prix two-stroke, and at around £50,000 all for half the price of a pukka works Superbike! On the bike's first outing at the Brands Hatch GSX-R Festival in August 2001, its first riders were none other than Kevin Schwantz, Pier-Francesco Chili, and Niall Mackenzie.

Mackenzie, reporting for *Two Wheels Only*

Mack enjoyed his time on the 1000. Litre machines will run in the British Superbike series from 2002. (John Noble)

magazine, was the first journalist to write about the new bike. He said: 'I've ridden a lot of GSX-R1000s, including superstockers and they feel like they're riding you around the circuit. This beast – with factory suspension and slicks – gives you a feeling of control, which is what you want on something with this much power. Power comes in at 7,000–8,000 revs, meaning you have more torque to play with than a Superbike and therefore you can ride it much more like a Ducati. Max power is quoted at 180, personally I reckon it's nearer 160 at the moment. On my first runs on the bike I could do a 48.6s lap of the Indy circuit and I was comfortable doing those times. Later in the day I rode John Crawford's spare GSX-R750 Superbike and was working hard to get down to low 48s and high 47s. That shows how impressive the 1000 is for a bike that had just begun to turn a wheel in anger.'

Denning too was impressed. 'On this initial test it didn't go faster than the 750 Superbike times-

wise, but it was very encouraging for us.' So encouraging that 2001 British Superbike champ John Reynolds decided to join the team riding the new bike for 2002, bringing him back into the Suzuki fold after a seven-year break. In an impressive line-up, 2001 British Supersport champ Karl Harris will join him. In early 2002 a test at the Almeria circuit underlined the potential of the machine, with Reynolds going quicker than he had on his Ducati around the Spanish circuit.

So, the GSX-R1000 is a true successor to the 1100's tag of ultimate sports machine, although the earlier bike's propensity for weight gain will surely not be replicated by the 1000, as the 'light is right' concept is too far ingrained in the brains of Japanese sports bike designers and the 1000 is destined for the racetrack. Whether or not the GSX-R1000 ingrains itself into the psyche of GSX-R fans around the world like the 1100 and 750 have remains to be seen.

Distant cousins

One machine that really deserves to be mentioned in the same breath as the GSX-R family is the Suzuki Hayabusa. The Hayabusa is not a GSX-R as such, it's a GSX1300R, the sporting moniker being dropped to illustrate a more sports-touring side to its nature. Whatever name it has, it still shares much with the GSX-R range, being the sportiest of the hyper-sports-tourers that can boast up to 170bhp and a 200mph (321.8kph) top speed. The GSX1300R was launched in 1999 and offered a real challenge to the likes of Honda's CBR1100XX Super Blackbird as ultimate speed king. Its name came from the Hayabusa, or Peregrine Falcon, which in its native Japan could dive to almost 200mph. Its looks came from somewhere else. 'A cross between a bull elephant and a cyclops,' according to Martin Child from *Bike* magazine. Still, its performance also came from another world. Later that year *Bike* would test the bike to 200.2mph (322.1kph), although when a picture of the speed was shown on the timing lights eagle-eyed readers spotted that the lights should have been calibrated two years earlier; a more normal figure is in the region of 185mph (297.7kph).

This amazing speed came from nothing that was technologically special or different from any other bike. It had a 1,298cc liquid-cooled inline four motor, equipped with ram-air (SRAD) and fuel injection.

Claimed output was 173bhp (129KW) at 9,800 revs, although when tested an average of around 150bhp (112KW) at the rear wheel was closer to the truth. The motor was unsurprisingly based on the more modern 750 than the earlier 1100s. The chassis had to be almost as powerful to keep all these horses in check. A beefy aluminium beam frame and chunky swingarm were 15 per cent stronger than the GSX-R750 of the time. Meanwhile suspension was 43mm fully-adjustable upside-down forks and a fully adjustable rear monoshock.

While nothing seemed revolutionary, what *did* seem to do the job were the aerodynamics. Starting right at the front with the sculptured mudguard, the Suzuki engineers spent hours in the wind tunnel in their search for the slipperiest shape imaginable. In fact, the Hayabusa is claimed to be the first motorcycle designed in the wind tunnel *with* a dummy rider on board for a human shape to be part of the drag equation as well.

And it wasn't simply an outright speedster, either. At the launch in Spain the Suzuki engineers said that the GSX1300R was 'at home on the road or track.' And to prove it they took the bike to the twisty Catalunya race circuit. *Bike* mag's Martin Child was impressed by how the big bike felt on the track: 'The Hayabusa is agile. Not 600 agile or even 1,000 agile, but the Hayabusa does better on the tack than it should.' Whatever speeds the Hayabusa was attaining, it was clear that this was a quick bike, in fact the quickest bike ever produced. Even with the launch of the Kawasaki ZX-12R a year later, the slippery aerodynamics of the 'Busa could push it to a higher top speed even if the outright power war was won on the dyno by the Kawasaki.

One machine that can claim perhaps even more direct lineage with the GSX-R series would be the Suzuki GSF1200 Bandit family. The original 1995 GSF600 Bandit took a novel approach to motorcycle marketing, if not building. Take an old motor (the venerable GSX-F 'Teapot' motor) and sling it in a steel perimeter frame, with budget forks, shock, and brakes. Leave out a fairing and cross a few zeros off the price. The Bandit was a revelation, selling like hot-cakes across Europe as well as battling with the likes of the mighty Honda FireBlade at the top of the sales charts in sportsbike-mad Blighty. If it could work for the middleweight class surely it could work in other classes, too? In fact, it already had. Suzuki had seen the whole 'Streetfighter' concept take off. This was where crashed sports bikes were deemed too expensive to repair on a 'panel for panel' basis. Instead, owners were sticking straight bars on the bikes and bug-eye headlights. Suzuki realised they could do the same as the Bandit, but with a bigger motor, thus making an out-of-the-box Streetfighter,

Suzuki's GSX1300R Hayabusa. While not a GSX-R, it owes a lot to the R's heritage. (Jason Critchell)

Suzuki's Bandit series used motors from the GSX-F600 for the Bandit 6 and the GSX-R1100 for the Bandit 12. Spot the difference? The 12 is on the left. (John Noble)

complete with zero miles on the clock, a full warranty, and without the pain of skinned knuckles or a box of bits perennially sitting in the garage.

There was only really one choice to power the Bandit – the GSX-R1100 motor. So, while the big GSX-R may have been dead, its heart was still beating. This heart wasn't the later liquid-cooled 16-valve four, instead it was the old oil/air-cooled mill, bored-out to 1,157cc and pumping out a respectable but not Earth-shattering 100 Euro and French-friendly bhp. Again, this clever combination of lots of performance and metal for little money made the GSF1200 Bandit in all its forms (faired or unfaired) into a clear winner, until other manufacturers jumped on the bandwagon. *Bike* magazine's Martin Child summed it up. The GSX-R fanatic and professional stunt rider used one as his long-termer for a year, demonstrating his skills at various shows on it, and reckoned: 'It's a straight from the crate stunt bike. Perfect.'

Suzuki's successful 1200 Bandit was not the only machine to use a version of the legendary 16-valve

inline four. In the late 1980s, the Suzuki GSX1100F was an attempt by the factory to produce a sports tourer able to take on the likes of the Honda CBR1000 and Kawasaki ZZ-R1100 family, using once more the heart of the GSX-R1100, in its 1,127cc version. Released in 1987, the machine looked a little like the 'Teapot' GSX600F and never really made a big hit with buyers, although it did offer good value compared to its rivals and featured a novel electric screen which could be adjusted at the touch of a button; and that engine, even in such uninspiring clothes, could still impress. As *Motorcycle International* said in a test against the ZZ-R and CBR: 'The motor is still impressive. This bike is a wolf in sheep's clothing.' The GSX1100F survived until being discontinued in 1996.

The Crescent Suzuki GSX-R750. £30,000 gets you this racetrack replica. (Jason Critchell)

Of Streetfighters and 7/11s

The GSX-R750 invented the race-replica class. Every sportsbike that followed it, and every sports bike fan, owes it a debt of gratitude. But through the years the impact of the GSX-R and its descendants has built up into something so much more substantial than that. So much so, that a completely different type of biker and bike was born. When GSX-Rs were crashed (and they often were) the price of rebuilding the bike back to standard in the late 1980s and 1990s, or claiming off the insurance to do so, was such that many owners simply didn't bother. Then they would take the bent clip-ons off the bike and put hi-rise or Renthal bars on it, making an already flighty machine even easier to wheelie. Damaged bodywork would be consigned to the bin, which presented the owners with a problem – there was now lots of frame and engine on show, so something had to be done. Frames would be polished, engines would receive anodised bolts, braided hoses, Some would go further… how does slipping a GSX-R1100 engine into a sweeter handling 750 frame sound? And then turbo it … or give it nitrous oxide…

Through this make-do-and-mend attitude, a new class of bikes and bikers was born, the 'Streetfighters'. And pretty soon make-do-and-mend became state-of-the-art, as Streetfighter machines became rolling works of art with specifications that would shame most production machines. Here's a selection of special GSX-Rs.

Suzuki GSX-R specials

Harris Magnum 4

The Harris brothers have been involved in racing for years and have a long history of building superb specials for the road. The original Magnum, based on an endurance-race trellis and unleashed onto the roads in 1979, was arguably the best-loved of the lot. The Harris Magnum 4 is ultimate Streetfighter cool, going as far as doing away with the standard double-cradle frame completely. Designed by Steve and Lester themselves, it was designed to 'look like an AC Cobra on two wheels!' Suzuki's oil-cooled GSX-R lump fits in the chassis – either the 1100 or 750cc engine, depending on budget. And here's where the Magnum scores. It's gonna cost to get that saucy frame wrapped around your GSX-R motor, but after that the chassis parts are down to whatever you can find in your local breakers or, if you're feeling flush, then Steve and Lester will be more than happy to send you a Harris catalogue, where you can spend to your heart's content on Öhlins this, Brembo that.

The frame dominates totally. On each side of the bike, a main tube of 1⅜-thick Renolds 531

The Harris Magnum 4 is as close as you can get to a 'factory' Streetfighter special. (Roland Brown)

curves out from the cylinder head, hugging the sides of the close-finned cylinder barrel on its way to the swingarm pivot. Another big tube runs near-vertically down to an engine-mount at the front of the cases. Narrower cross-members join the two, completing a ladder-like pattern that is similar in appearance to that of the Mk 1 and 2 Magnums. (The Mk 3, released in 1985, had a more conventional twin-cradle frame.) The swingarm is nothing like the earlier versions, being an aluminium deltabox-style construction, with massive strengthening on top, that works a vertically-mounted Öhlins shock. Front suspension, like much of the Magnum's detailing, depends on customer preference. The Mk 4's wheelbase is 1,372mm (54in), considerably shorter than the 1994

vintage GSX-R750's 1,420mm (55.9in) and dinky-sized in comparison with the Eleven's 1,465mm (57.7in). Weight is around 181kg (398.7lb).

The frame itself is probably heavier than stock, but the Magnum's no-frills format and simple four-into-one exhaust system save precious pounds. The deliciously-sculpted alloy fuel tank retains the family look, as does the typically minimal fibreglass seat unit (which holds the battery in the seat hump). Previous Magnums had fairings, when such things were novelties, but the Mk 4 makes do with just a pair of frog-eye headlights ahead of its clip-ons, and with no more than an oil cooler to keep the flies off the engine. In Harris tradition, the Magnum is produced essentially as a chassis

Mark Moisan's GSX-R1100 is a beast. How else would 414.4bhp feel? (Roland Brown)

kit comprising frame, swingarm, rear shock and linkages, petrol tank, seat unit, footrests, and rear-brake master cylinder, plus various brackets, engine-plates, and bearings. To that list must be added not only the engine, electrics, carbs, exhaust system, and forks, but also wheels, brakes, yokes, handlebars, oil cooler (the tuned bike runs two), clocks, and all the hundred and one odds and sods that go into constructing a complete motorcycle.

The result is something that, despite coming from a kit, still has its own individuality and a handy handling advantage over the 1100. Many Harris Magnum owners ended up tuning them, or boring them out to 1,340cc, fitting nitrous, turbos, Cosworth pistons … the sky's the limit.

Mark Moisan GSX-R1100 Turbo

Big numbers are what Mark's 1100 turbo is about. It's geared for 196mph (315.4kph) at the 11,500rpm redline, runs 19psi of boost, and tags the rev-limiter at just over 200mph (321.8kph). With the same boost and more gearing it's been timed at 229.65mph (369.51kph). Want more big numbers? Then how does an incredible 414.4bhp sound? It all adds up to the small number of 9.63 seconds down the standing start quarter mile and the big 164.12mph (264.07kph) terminal speed. The most impressive thing is that Mark's bike is his daily transport, with him putting 700 miles (1,126km) on the thing during Daytona in 1994.

After buying the bike new in 1990, he spent a

couple of years tuning it and strapping on a nitrous system, but after three years he got bored with refilling nitrous bottles. Nine months and a considerable amount of money later, a Rayjay 300-series turbocharger sat in front of the engine behind a big K&N filter, force-feeding modified standard 36mm Mikuni carbs via Moisan's own plumbing arrangement. Capacity of the oil/air-cooled 16-valve motor remains at 1,127cc, and a surprising amount is stock, including the crankshaft, camshafts, con-rods, and inlet valves. The original pistons have been machined to reduce compression ratio to 8.5:1. Non-standard parts include stainless steel exhaust valves, heavy-duty engine studs, S&R ignition advancer, and MDS fuel pump. The clutch is a lock-up unit from MTC (using centrifugal force to locate positively at speed), running slightly stiffer than standard springs. The gearbox has been heat-treated and undercut by Florida firm MRE. The standard oil cooler was moved to a new position under the seat, to make room for a big Spearco intercooler up front, fed via a ram-air slot in the nose of the Kawasaki ZZ-R1100 fairing.

Custom-painted to match the standard GSX-R tailpiece, and wearing a slightly taller than stock screen, the fairing blends in to give a deceptively ordinary overall appearance. Moisan also added a few chassis mods. Stock forks (unlike most markets, the US didn't get upside-down legs in 1990) are fitted with Progressive Suspension springs and a Sims & Rohm brace; the rear shock is from Öhlins. Wheels are standard 17-inchers. The front brake is uprated with 330mm floating discs and four-pot calipers from Performance Machine, plumbed-in with a GSX-R750 master cylinder from a 1994 vintage machine. Add a smattering of titanium fasteners and the end result is a bike that weighs 228kg (502.2lb) dry, a little more than standard, and produces well over

twice as much horsepower. Whereas a stock GSX-R11 is running out of steam at 170mph (273.5kph), Mark's bike accelerates from that speed almost as strongly as it had from 120mph (193.1kph). Impressive for a well-used bike. 'It has been phenomenal – I've never had a single major problem. I ride it about twice a week on average, and when I go out on it I do 70 or 80-mile stints. This bike's no trailer queen.'

Joel Broida's GSX-R1340

Being a multi-millionaire, Joel Broida is going to be able to splash out on his pride and joy. It looks like just another slightly tarted-up GSX-R750. But far from being a mere 750 with shiny wheels and a four-into-one, the Suzuki is a 1,340cc monster that made over 200bhp with nitrous oxide fitted and can run a 9.87s standing quarter. Joel got Lee Shierts of Lee's Cycle Service in San Diego to build the bike for him. Lee – a racer himself – loves horsepower, and Joel's machine is an interpretation of his race bike for the street. The capacity hike comes from fitting a GSX1100F engine with 85mm Cosworth pistons, running 11.6:1 compression ratio to allow pump fuel without detonation. (The race bike runs as high as 13.3:1.) Stage two Yoshimura cams, big valves, and heavy-duty springs with titanium retainers liven up the roadster's top-end. Lee ported the head, modified the combustion chambers, and polished the cases, also fitting heavy-duty cylinder studs and Carrillo rods and a one-piece aluminium head gasket that he had specially made.

The crank and gearbox are standard; the clutch uses Barnett plates plus a GSX600 cable-operation set-up in place of the standard hydraulics. Carbs are filterless 41mm smoothbore Keihins, tugged by a quick-action

It looks standard, with 750 stickers and all, but Joel Broida's GSX-R is a 1,340cc beast. (Roland Brown)

throttle; the pipe is a D&D four-into-one. An Earl's auxiliary oil cooler sits beneath the slatted seat hump, and there's a neat polished alloy breather box in the crook of the rear subframe on the right. Nitrous oxide gives an extra 50bhp or so at the touch of a button, but Joel had it disconnected as he reckons it's just too over the top for the street.

The chassis is basically a stock 1991 model GSX-R750 fitted with an Öhlins shock, Performance Machine cast iron front discs, and the same firm's aluminium wheels. The bike is torquey and smooth, pulling from as low as 2,000rpm in top gear. Max speed is around 190mph (305.7kph). Joel reckons the GSX-R's undramatic appearance adds extra spice when he pulls alongside some unsuspecting FireBlade pilot on the freeway and cracks the loud handle to send the Suzuki steaming off into the distance. Even the GSX-R's '750' stickers are still in place, which must make this some kind of ultimate street-sleeper.

Mark Moisan GSX-R750 Turbo

When the WT came out in 1996 people loved it, but while being a revvy little beast it still didn't have the knockout punch of the FireBlade, ZX-9R, or the later YZF-R1. What you need is a bike with a horseshoe in its boxing glove – and this is it. American Turbo Systems boss Mark Moisan took the experience of building his superb 1100 and set it another challenge: to give the water-cooled 750 a real shot in the arm. The Schwitzer turbo lurking beneath the fairing is rated at 275 cubic feet per minute, enough to lift the GSX-R750's peak output to over 180bhp with the maximum 0.55bar (8psi) of boost. But Moisan says that's just too mental for street use. The kit's standard setting will be 0.4bar (5.8psi), good for 150–160bhp on pump petrol. Moisan adds: 'The kit includes a switch that will give a choice between 5.8 and 8psi. On the higher setting the bike is totally unrideable, but that's what some people want!' The kit, which in 1998 cost around

**Mark Moisan and his GSX-R750 turbo. £3,000 gets you
165bhp.** (Roland Brown)

£3,000, comes complete with turbocharger,
intercooler, boost gauge, and a stainless steel
exhaust system with carbon end can. As well as
all necessary fitting brackets it also includes
jets with which to modify the Suzuki's 39mm
Mikuni carbs.

An important component of the kit was a 1mm
thicker base gasket, necessary to reduce the
GSX-R's compression ratio from the standard
11.8:1 to a detonation-preventing 10.5:1. Despite
the GSX-R750WT's compact nature, the turbo
and its assorted parts tuck away so efficiently
that nobody glancing at the bike would suspect
that it had anything naughty up its skirt. Even
when you climb aboard and fire it up, the Suzuki
feels deceptively ordinary. Even below 6,000 revs
it feels like any other 750, but after that it hauls
you towards the horizon like no other 750 on
Earth. That twin-beam GSX-R frame is rigid, and

the suspension, brakes, and tyres are well
capable of handling the extra power. On the
dyno and at 0.4bar it produces no less than
164.8bhp (approx 50bhp up on stock). Just
the job for kicking sand in the faces of all those
Yam R1s.

Tryphonos GSX-R750

This machine is perhaps the most bizarre looking
GSX-R-based machine ever built. Following the
early nineties trend of looking for an alternative to
the front fork, a few production machines – the
Bimota Tesi and the Yamaha GTS1000A – tried to
lure us away from convention. The Tryphonos
Alternative Geometry (TAG for short) Suzuki
GSX-R750 was one of those machines, but on a
smaller scale. Designed and built by Mike
Tryphonos, it, like the Tesi, began as a degree

It looks like nothing on Earth... but believe it or not there is a 750L motor of 1990 vintage in there. (Roland Brown)

project. Mike spent the next five years perfecting it before offering the chassis as a kit for GSX-R owners. Understandably, Tryphonos was inspired by alternative machines including the Elf endurance racers of the early 1980s, and came up with his own variation on the Difazio-type forkless front-end theme.

The TAG's front-end works in a similar way to that of the Tesi. In each case steering is achieved by turning the front wheel on a bearing inside its hub. Differences include the fact that the TAG's steering linkage is simpler. The handlebar forms the top of a large tubular-steel T shape, the vertical column of which runs neatly down behind the exhaust downpipes. From the bottom of that column, a rod transmits the rider's steering input horizontally to the front wheel hub. Only two spherical bearings are needed, unlike the Tesi, which uses a considerably more complicated link between handlebars and hub. This prototype was based on a 1990 750L, standard apart from Ramair filters, a Dynojet carb kit, and a four-into-one exhaust system, made by Tryphonos from two Yoshimura pipes and topped with a carbon can from Race Products. The prototype uses heaps of carbon, its unpainted bodywork consisting of a fairing designed for a Yamaha FZR400 (holding a tiny headlight from a Honda C90) and a single-seat unit made for a TZ250. Weight was 168kg (370lb) dry, a handy 25kg (55.1lb) less than a standard 750L and 40kg (88.1lb) down on the water-cooled 750W.

So does it work? Roland Brown had a go. He said: 'At very slow speeds the handlebars – which pivoted slightly up-and-down, as well as to left and right in the conventional fashion – waggled about in a disconcertingly vague way. That made slow-speed manoeuvring difficult, as did the severely limited steering lock. But once I was much above walking pace that imprecise feeling disappeared and the TAG very quickly felt like a normal bike. Mike had got the suspension

pretty well right judging by the way the TAG felt firm yet did a good job of gliding over minor bumps. On tight roads the TAG really began to show its value, helped by a wheelbase that at 1,410mm is 5mm shorter than the stock L. It felt as taut, light and manoeuvrable as a good 400cc supersports bike. On the roundabout where we did the pics I set a personal record of one-and-a-half laps with my knee on the ground all the way.'

A trip to Brands Hatch to really test the bike's handling ended in disaster. 'I couldn't wait to get out on the track and show up a few of those old-fashioned bikes with forks,' said Roland. 'But then I crashed it when I lost the front end at a spot where resurfacing had left quite a large step down in the tarmac. Mike was pretty upset, more because he felt the bike had failed than because he'd have to fix it, but basically the crash was down to me simply being tempted to ride it too fast. Despite the crash I was mighty impressed with the TAG.' The bike was soon rebuilt and was actually raced at the Isle of Man TT races that year. The kits cost £10,000 and included everything on the bike bar engine and electrics. Even in 1995 that was a lot of money to replace a set of forks that still worked well enough for most of us. Perhaps one day…

Bimota SB7

Stretching back to the first ever Bimota, the SB2, this Italian firm has had strong links with the Suzuki factory. The SB7 came along in early 1994 and looked like the most gorgeously crafted race replica ever, even knocking the donor GSX-R750SP into a cocked hat. Developed for the racetrack, one major difference is that instead of using carbs, the 750 got its gas via a TDD fuel injection engine management system that monitored revs, ignition advance, ambient air pressure, and the temperatures of both intake air and coolant. The 749cc SP unit itself was very similar to the standard water-cooled 16-valver, the main difference being a close-ratio gearbox. To make the SB7 engine cocktail, Bimota added its own camshafts, each giving more lift and duration, plus a set of colder plugs and a slinky exhaust system that ended up with twin alloy cans tucked away inside the sexy self-supporting carbon-fibre seat unit. The twin-spar alloy frame linked the steering head and swingarm pivot directly, in what Bimota called 'Straight Connection Technology'.

Suspension at the rear was a horizontally laid out Ohlins shock on the right of the bike, multi-adjustable and working the swingarm via a

linkage. Up front sat a pair of 46mm front forks, made by Paioli to Bimota's specification, which incorporated sliders constructed from a composite of aluminium and carbon fibre. It weighed in at 186kg (409.7lb) dry, 22kg (48.5lb) down on the standard GSX-R. Its wheelbase was just 1,390mm (54.7in), 45mm shorter than the Suzuki's. Provided the revs were kept up, its fuel injection gave a superbly crisp response that had the Bimota screaming towards a top speed somewhere in excess of the GSX-R's 160mph (257.4kph).

Its big horses lived at the top end of the rev range, with the claimed max output of 132bhp arriving, like the standard GSX-R's claimed 118bhp, at 11,500rpm. The close-ratio box made it easy to keep the motor on the boil, and on the right road the Seven felt fast enough to live with just about anything. The Bim certainly had to be ridden with a fair degree of aggression, because it refused to pull from below 5,000rpm once out of its tall (but not RC45 tall) first gear, merely stuttering and croaking until it reached that figure. Strong acceleration didn't arrive until 8,000rpm. Being a Bimota, the SB7 was pricey. A whopping £17,000 on the road made the bike almost as dear as Honda's RC45.

As if the 750 version wasn't enough, Bimota also produced the SB6 at the same time, which was visually similar to the SB7 but featured the water-cooled GSX-R 1100 motor, carbs, and was £1,000 cheaper. Sadly, in the hands of road testers Bimota's fuel injection system on both machines proved problematical, although when they worked, they were sublime.

With the original total of 200 machines being built for homologation in World Superbikes, the aim was to replicate the glory days of Virginio Ferrari's Formula One title of 1987. Sadly, the machine never made an impact, despite securing the service of Terry Rymer. In the end the racing project was stillborn. The SB7 was discontinued at the end of 1996, while the SB6 and later SB6-R carried on until 1999. In a happy end to the Bimota/Suzuki race story, the Italian factory did return to the top of the podium, courtesy of the SB8-R. This was another race-bred machine, featuring Suzuki TL1000R V-twin power. In the hands of the mercurial Anthony Gobert it won the second World Superbike leg at Phillip Island in damp conditions. The manager of the team was Ferrari, who'd won the F1 title all those years before.

Crescent Suzuki GSX-R750

Thirty thousand pounds buys you what you see on page 128, a near-as-dammit replica of the machine that John Crawford raced in the UK's domestic Superbike series in 2001. So similar is it to JC's race bike that it's only the headlight peeping out from behind the number board and the tax disc slapped on to the carbon-fibre SRAD intake trunking that really gives the game away. *Two Wheels Only* magazine's Niall Mackenzie got to test it just weeks after racing Crawford's spare 750 Superbike at Knockhill and he was amazed at the similarities. The first big similarity is the fact that this machine is a track bike first and foremost. Up against the stocker on the road, it's a poor relation, wheezing and farting until 8,000 revs when the bike suddenly kicks into the Mr Hyde side of its character. The Crescent bike makes the standard machine feel like a pussycat in comparison, and Niall reckoned the top-end wasn't far shy of the racer.

All told the Crescent machine makes 139bhp (104kW) at 12,600rpm thanks to some serious bits of kit inside the motor. The engine breathes through a BMC race filter which mixes with fuel pumped in by a re-mapped ECU and fuel injection system (and with Cresecent's race history with these bikes they know just what they're doing). The head is gas flowed and skimmed to allow the compression ratio to be raised up to 14.2:1 (the stock bike is just 12.0:1).

Bimota's gorgeous SB7. The curvy bodywork hid a fuel-injected 750SP motor. (Roland Brown)

You've also got Yoshimura cams, a factory replica radiator, and those carbon air-scoops. All this power is then transmitted through a Yoshi close-ratio six-speed gearbox, barking through a Yoshimura Tri-Oval pipe. The bike also has a factory quick-shifter to help you get the most out of that all-or-nothing powerband.

On the chassis side of things the frame is standard, but the swingarm is replaced with one straight from the Crescent factory bike. The rear shock and front forks are factory race-spec Showas – you don't buy these, no matter how much money you have; the fact that this machine wears them is purely because of the access the team has to Showa's finest. The forks are held in place by factory triple clamps and a top yoke from Crawford's number one race bike. To prevent the beast getting the shakes at speed you've also got an Öhlins steering damper. Marchesini race wheels are used front and rear, along with AP Lockheed six-pot caliper brakes. The tank is an alloy race item, and the fairing and bodywork is a carbon/Kevlar version of the swoopy original. For your hands and feet you have factory clip-ons and Yoshimura rear-sets.

The whole bike looks so much like the race machine it's just untrue. I can't believe I'm going to write this, but at £30,000 this is a bargain, a mere snip, if the rumoured £100,000 price-tag of the race bike is to be believed!

Stunt kings

Pretty much simultaneously across Europe in the early 1990s, a new breed of GSX-R rider was coming to the fore. With a huge excess of power available from the GSX-R engine, anybody with a half-decent sense of balance could wheelie their bike. And, with a bit of practice and a dollop more balance, these same people found they could engage in massive rolling burnouts which, while not being the best thing for the environment, could be most entertaining to watch. Add in six-pot brakes that would get the tail wagging in the air at the mere thought of a tug on the lever and you had the recipe for a stunt display.

In the UK the man who started the trend was Liverpudlian Gary Rothwell. 'I had one of the original slabby GSX-R1100s,' he recalls. 'The motor was just amazing, so much power. The first time I actually did a proper show, though, was, I think, around 1993 at the Day of Champions at the British GP at Donington Park, on a bike given to me by Nick Coulton of West Coast motorcycles. Really after that first show the thing just took off.' Since then Gary's name has been linked with that of the GSX-R and the 1100 in particular. It's not surprising he loves them. 'In the nine years or so I've been stunting I've only had two engines go pop, although I only really count the one, as it was new at the time. That's really impressive. One bike I even had for six years before anything major went wrong with it and it had to be rebuilt. People see what you do

with the bikes in a show and think that they get rebuilt after every show or so, but that's not the case. They're bullet-proof, although you can get through a few second gears as they take a lot of punishment during wheelies.'

Over the years Gary's display became more and more polished. The crowds got bigger – and further away, as pretty soon he was putting on shows in the USA – and more and more riders wanted to emulate him. Gary now owns a motorcycle shop in his home town of Liverpool and still pulls some outrageous stunts either on his turbo Hayabusa or his trusty GSX-R1100.

Martin Child was another talented rider who turned to stunting when he saw Gary perform. After buying a 1991 GSX-R750L, he was perhaps the only person to convert it to Streetfighter style without having first crashed it! An 1100 motor was soon shoehorned inside the frame, giving him the power he needed, the name 'Wild' was inserted before Child, and he was soon entertaining the crowds. He recalls: 'That 750L that I bought in 1993 changed my life. I got hooked on stunting and pretty soon I just had to practice everyday. Two massive dents in the tank showed where my backside had been during on-the-tank wheelies [a tube was soon inserted in the tank to stop it collapsing entirely], and I was soon strapping push-bike tyres on the side of the bike while I practised "surfing", or standing on the tank while the bike went on its merry way. I love that bike and I love GSX-Rs in general. For me, they sum up a particular type of biker. Mad and bad!'

When, finally, the old GSX-R was retired in favour of a Suzuki Bandit 1200, Wild Child did what any self-respecting GSX-R fanatic would do and brought it in from the garage and had it mounted on the wall in his sitting room! Pretty soon there were a host of copy-cat wannabe stuntmen honing their art, many on GSX-Rs. Eventually, a European Stunt Championship was set up to cater for this booming trend.

Old habits die hard with 'Wild' Child. 750, 1100, 7/11, or this TTS special 750, he'll still wheelie it. (*Bike* magazine)

In France, too, the GSX-R, and the 1100 in particular, were marked as something special. Despite the fact that all French machines were restricted to just 100bhp they sold well, with the 1100 alone selling more than 17,000 units in the decade or so it was available.

Nicolas Sauhet is a life-long GSX-R fan, making the trip over to the UK especially for the GSX-R Festival. 'I love the GSX-R range. Sometimes you loved it despite the fact that it could be difficult. The 1100 was sometimes like a truck to handle – especially the 1989 model! You needed to fight to make it turn although its suspension was virtually perfect. To be fast on it, you had to be authoritarian and gifted. Why was the 1100 such a success? The Suzuki owes it to an incredible engine which had five gears, bad manners, unfiltered vibrations and a torque never known before on any four-cylinder bike. The GSXR 1100 became famous and a whole generation of bikers dreamt of it. When de-restricted, if you wanted to or not, if you knew how to wheely or not, it didn't matter, because the beast raised its front wheel all the time. The dealers were mad because of the number of fork seals they had to replace, seals which would explode at every violent landing. More than once in a French Suzuki dealership the phrase: "No sir, I swear I don't do wheelies" was heard! Many bikes were badly crashed after non-mastered wheelies, but everybody enjoyed its de-restricted 143bhp – even the notorious "Black Prince", who was filmed as he went around the Paris ring-road in the morning, with the needle of the tachometer at around 280kph [174mph]!'

The French, with their unique sense of style, soon began to modify there own machines. Some would look similar to the Streetfighters and 7/11s seen in the UK, but would have Gallic extras, such as micro headlights, tailpiece undertrays, and MIG or Devil exhausts. In readers' surveys about the first GSX-R1100, more than 70 per cent of owners said they had de-restricted their bike. Now, almost all the old GSX-Rs you see in Paris have open pipes and are de-restricted, which was a simple job on the earlier machines.

'This explains why the '92 GSX-R750 and 1993 water-cooled GSX-R1100 did not sell well,' explains Nicolas. 'They were too expensive to de-restrict. The same happened with the Yamaha

Whatever the GSX-R model, it'll do stunts. This is a smiling
Kevin Carmichael – the European Stunt Champion – on his
converted GSX-R1000. (Suzuki UK)

combine sports and real life. The GSXR always
sold very well in France for a number of reasons.
Firstly, image is always important to us and the
GSX-R had the perfect image. Secondly, Suzukis
at the time were around five to ten per cent
cheaper than the competition. We like endurance
races and Suzukis always did very well in
endurance racing – the Kawasaki ZXR sold very
well for the same reasons.'

All GSX-R1100s sold in France were restricted
to that country's 100bhp law. In the UK, early
G/H/J 1100s from 1986 to 1988 had restrictors in
the exhausts, which when removed or swapped
for a full system liberated the full amount of
power. It's similar with the K–N 1100s of 1989 to
1992. The exhaust system would keep power at
125bhp – a new exhaust does the job, or the
original item from a US-spec machine. Otherwise
it's a difficult job of drilling the tailpipe.

The last of the many 1100s to reach UK shores
in 1995 and 1996 were also restricted, but this
time to 'only' 133 claimed bhp. To get an extra
22bhp from the GSX-R1100WS, you had to
remove the restrictor plates which sat across the
inlet webs which restricted flow to the carbs by
around two-thirds. An Allen key, some ring
spanners, and a couple of screwdrivers, along
with two hours' work shifting the tank, left-hand
fairing panel, and airbox, would soon see the
removal of the web in each of the inlet stubs. The
bike also had a rev-limiter in third gear which was
also easily bypassed by looking under the left-
hand side panel for a pink wire. Disconnect the
bullet connector in the middle and voila! Around
155 claimed bhp and a bike which is transformed
from 6,000 revs upwards.

With age, many early GSX-R owners are now
looking to leave their machine standard, as the
bike is rightfully considered a modern classic.
Tony Scragg owns a 1986 GSX-R750G and this
machine has withstood the ravages of time well,
getting more than its fair share of looks from the
gathered masses at the inaugural GSX-R Festival

FZR1000 and Honda CBR1000. They did not sell
well because they respected the law too much!
Cams, exhaust pipes and more had to be
changed for de-restriction. Even restricted the 11
had a better engine than the 750. In France the
750 was used for racing or bought by younger
riders. It was pure sport, while the 11 could

Tony Scragg and his mint 1986 750G. (Roland Brown)

Tony's 750G can still go around corners 15 years later. (Roland Brown)

Peter Small at the 1998 TT. He would later ride this same machine around Europe on holiday. (Phil Masters)

at Brands Hatch. It's clear from what he says that he has an affection for the GSX-R. 'I love it! After my previous GS750 it was a revelation in terms of handling, performance, and weight. It does take a bit of work to get the best out of the performance, which kicks in at 7,000, then its pure enjoyment to the 11,000 redline. Having said that, it is well behaved around town as well.

'I had the chance to ride a 2001 model a few months before the GSX-R day, and what a difference there was. As well as the obvious 16 years of extra development (more power, more brakes, smoothness, handling) the bike is a totally different experience. With my bike you feel like you are sitting in it, low down behind the tank and fairing. With the new bike you are perched right on top – still a great buzz though! Mostly I use the bike solo for shortish rides but I do carry a pillion at times and it's OK for both – though not as roomy in the saddle as the old GS. Distance is no problem either, though the footrests are quite high and took a bit of getting used to at first. Ground clearance is massive. I haven't even come close to getting anything on the bike scraping the road! I have had a couple of scary moments on very rough road surfaces whilst accelerating fast by getting a couple of tank slappers, but I came through OK both times.

Roland Brown on the 1996 GSX-R. He rates the Gixxer 750 as the second most influential bike in the last century. (Roland Brown)

Perhaps I could do with a steering damper, which got fitted as standard to the later ones.

'Reliability has been good, a reputation which is justified for the GSX-R. I've heard that the rear suspension bushes can wear, but so far so good for me. Tyres are getting harder to find for the 18-inch wheels, or at least the choice is a bit limited. It's not such a problem, as I do about 1,500 miles a year. In summary the bike is great fun – plenty fast enough for me, cheap to insure with a classic policy, spares seem reasonably priced, and I enjoy the social scene with the Suzuki Owners' Club.'

Tony's immaculate GSX-R750G featured in an article where one old warrior from the past, the GSX-R, met another, journalist Roland Brown. Dear old Roland got a bit dewy-eyed when he threw a leg over Tony's bike for *Classic*

Motorcycle Mechanics. 'My adrenaline was pumping as I carved my way through the next roundabout with my knee on the ground, fondly imagining that I was back in the mid-80s and that the bike I was riding was the fastest thing on two wheels. The reality is, of course, very different and any of the modern crop of 600cc supersport bikes with their 120bhp engines and fat radial tyres would make mincemeat of the old warrior, but it was good to discover that the first GSX-R still punches hard, despite its age.'

Buying early models of the GSX-R range comes with the same warning that could be applied to buying any 'modern classic' sportsbike. You may have the best will in the world to look after it, but the several owners before you may not have had 'classic' status in mind when they were thrashing round on it.

Check for all the usual signs of abuse. A proliferation of lockwire could mean the bike had a spell on a racetrack, as does spanking new bodywork on a scruffier-looking chassis. Shocks and suspension will have seen years of abuse, so check to see if it works properly; if not, then budget for replacement. Remember that the early 1990s 750 and 1100 models benefited (or suffered from, depending on your point of view) suspension that was so adjustable you had something like a million different possible settings. So, it may just be set up badly.

Early GSX-Rs did suffer on the quality of finish front. Machines from the early 1990s on had much improved build quality, so bear that in mind when you're looking to buy. You may have to see more early GSX-Rs to find the one you want, but buying through the Suzuki Owners' Club, or the proliferation of websites dedicated to the cult of the GSX-R, could help you find the cherished machine you're after or at least help you find original spares for your bike. Remember, the GSX-R750 and 1100 have been around for so long there's a huge amount of parts on the market, so that's an advantage. Just make sure you know exactly what make and model you are looking at.

With so many versions produced over so many years, it's hard to pinpoint any particular weaknesses. Flexy wheels on the original 750 model, along with self-unscrewing oil filters (too small threads were to blame) and tales of three-figure tank-slappers, merge with tales of the 1100's massive weight gain, more tank slappers, and scary, top-heavy handling. Obviously, with time the machine has improved, but with the latest model of GSX-R, be it the 600, 750, or 1000, you're looking at a machine which is still true to the original concept – race-replica – and as such it deserves respect every time you throw a leg over it.

When you've made up your mind and bought a GSX-R, congratulate yourself – you're part of a fraternity. You're a GSX-R owner and therefore a breed apart. Taking the GSX-R to heart has proved to be a global phenomenon and has thrown up a number of characters. Take, for example, a man known only as 'Anders', who, when the snow and ice were at their coldest in his native Sweden, decided to whack a pair of studded motocross tyres on his GSX-R1100, dress up warm, and go for a ride. He recorded a top speed of around 135mph (217kph) on the ice! Our GSX-R-loving friends in northern Europe are full of such stories, and one to perhaps better that comes from – where else – the United States of America.

Peter Small is about as unlikely looking a hooligan as you could find. Now in his 50s, Pete has spent many of those years in a saddle looking for some action. Back in 1998, at 51 years young, he decided to go to Europe on his GSX-R750 to find some. Not only would he be touring Europe on his supersport machine (which at the time was 8,500 miles old) he would also be entering the toughest pure roads race of them all – the Isle of Man TT. Loaded down with everything he needed for the trip, Pete rode from his home in Idaho to Vancouver in Canada, where he loaded his GSX-R up for the freight flight to the UK. After picking it up at Gatwick, Pete spent three days touring Wales before getting on a ferry at Liverpool and setting sail for the Isle of Man, where he and his GSX-R were entered for the Formula One and Production Class races.

In his cool American drawl, Pete would tell anyone who'd listen to him why he entered the races. 'My street riding back home is so similar to the TT races, I think. My friends, my son, and I would do around 300 to maybe 500 miles a day on the wonderful roads of Idaho – the last State of the Union where there's no official speed limit. Sometimes we'd even ride into Canada. There are some great roads on the American continent.'

Classic clout – the GSX-R1100 motor

If there was a prize for 'Motor of the Millennium' for motorcycles the winner would have to be the oil/air-cooled mill from the GSX-R1100. In its various forms it's powered not just road-going GSX-Rs, but drag bikes, sidecar outfits, hill-climbers, grass-track outfits, micro-light aircraft, and small race cars. The 16-valve inline four is quite simply unburstable, when looked after properly, and daft figures of 300bhp (224kW) or more are achievable with the right sort of tuning.

Stage I

The first stage of tuning improves the 'breathing' of the engine. You do this by changing the exhaust, air filter, and jetting. Many firms make full-system exhausts or slip-on end-cans for the GSX-R, but remember that the early 1100 had a one-piece exhaust, so a slip-on is no use. High-flow air filters unsurprisingly let more air into the motor. Some machines sport individual foam filters which can give jetting problems, so always ask at a reputable tuning house what they find works best – remember, they see thousands of bikes like yours on their dyno every year. A jetting kit should help up the power as well as throttle response. You may also consider an ignition advance unit, which alters the ignition by about 5°. With all these mods you'd be looking at an increase of between 5–15bhp (4–12kW.)

Stage II

Porting the cylinder-head enlarges and reshapes the inlet and exhaust channels to improve flow. The combustion chamber can also be reshaped to improve flow and combustion. Porting the head gives mainly top-end power, but a good job will see increases in the whole rpm register. Next is to skim the head. That is to remove a thin layer of metal from the sealing surface on the head. That allows an increase in the compression ratio of the engine, which means more power, although you have to carefully calculate the compression ratio so that it does not get so high that it could damage the engine. Compression ratio also depends on what fuel you run. With 98 octane fuel you can run about 12.0:1 safely. Another thing to check is valve to piston clearance. One thing to remember when skimming is that the camshaft timing is altered, so you should buy adjustable cam sprockets (although some home-tuners modify their own). The first generation of the GSX-R1100 (1986–8) has small 34mm carbs. You can replace these with carbs from later GSX-R models or with aftermarket flat-slide items. The advantage of flat-

slide carbs is much increased airflow and greatly improved throttle response, although sometimes at the expense of mid-range response. Replacing ignition coils and wires with aftermarket ones can also help, especially following major head re-work. With these mods you will be looking at a further 10–20 bhp (7.5–15kW.)

Stage III

This stage will see you changing the camshafts and valves in the motor. Camshafts with a different profile enable the valves to lift more and stay open for longer. Increasing valve diameter also increases airflow. Another effective way of getting more power is putting more cee cees into the engine in the first place, and the robust 1100 motor has been increased in capacity to up to 1,300cc. Roughly speaking a ten per cent increase in volume gives around ten per cent more torque and five per cent more bhp. Anything more than around 1,230cc and you'd need to look at aftermarket engine internals to soak up the extra power. Done properly, these mods will see a further 15–50bhp, depending on how far you've bored it out and what camshafts you're using. Eight-times sidecar champ Steve Webster uses a bored-out GSX-R1100 motor, which with an off-the-shelf Wiseco piston kit is pumping out over 200bhp (149kW) with little effect on reliability.

TTS Engineering have been associated with Suzukis for years in the UK, looking after the machines raced by the Crescent Suzuki team in the British Superbike Championship. In 1997 they modified a GSX-R1100W to produce 190bhp (142kW) with 106lb ft (143Nm) of torque. To do this the cylinders were bored by 4mm to allow the use of 79.5mm pistons. The engine was stroked by 3mm to give 1,251cc. Carrillo rods were used, the head was flowed, and a stage 2 Yoshimura cams and valve spring kit was fitted, along with Keihin 41mm flat-slide carbs with open bellmouths. Engine compression was 12.8:1 and the whole thing breathed through a Yoshimura four-two-one pipe. *Performance Bikes* tested the machine and said: 'So what happens when the wrist and tendons move in anger? This GSX-R f**ks off, that's what!'

Turbo

Turbos use a turbine driven by exhaust gases to ram more air into the motor. GSX-R1100s using this form of forced induction can easily make 250bhp (187kW), although you'd have to strengthen con rods, crankshaft, and clutch to be able to use that power effectively. The sort of plain daft figures people can get from once-standard motors is illustrated by the much-modified GSX-R1100 which was at the 1998 Brute Horsepower Shoot-out at Daytona. This machine 'only' made 429bhp (320kW) at the back wheel. I say 'only' because it was beaten by a Kawasaki ZZ-R1100 which made 494.4bhp (369kW) and was clocked at 230.7mph (370kph)!

In 1997, *Superbike* magazine wanted to find the fastest non-turbo, non-nitrous bike in the UK and – unsurprisingly – the majority of those taking part were GSX-R1100-based. The most powerful was a much-modified GSX-R1100K, owned by Allistair Cook, which had a rear-wheel output of 185bhp (138kW). The first 180mph (289.6kph) run of the day went to another GSX-R1100, Andy Booth's 1,216cc K-model, but the ultimate winner was a Kawasaki ZX-9R Ninja, which benefited from better aerodynamics as well as a couple of years' worth of development, even if it lost out to the GSX-Rs on power output. While the 1100 motor – and the earlier oil/air-cooled ones especially – have a reputation for tunability, so do all the various GSX-R models. The latest water-cooled, beam-framed 750WT machine can easily be tuned to give anything from 120 to 140bhp (90 to 104kW). The 1996 TTS-tuned WT Crescent race bike campaigned by Ian Cobby and Paul Denning was pumping out 147bhp – impressive considering the size of their effort and lack of factory backing, although ultimately a few bhp down on the opposition of the time. TTS offered similar tunes to road-riding GSX-R owners, too. Many preferred to 'tune' the handling of the more flighty models of the GSX-R750 family. For example, many owners of the 1996 WT fitted a steering damper and added two links to the chain to max-out the wheelbase, giving the machine a dollop more stability.

Still, he craved a few of the sorts of roads that Europe could offer and wanted to see them the only way he knew how: from the saddle of his GSX-R. With the bike groaning under the weight of his kit and looking like 'a pregnant ant' according to Pete, he set out on his adventure. With his stock GSX-R pumping out no more than around 100bhp (75KW) he still managed to notch up a fastest lap of 106mph (170.5kph) in the Proddie race, with an average of 104mph (167.3kph). And those laps were set when he was still in pain from the earlier F1 race, where he ran off the road at Sulby as he attempted to outbrake a guy who'd been holding him up. 'Man, I went down the slip-road and didn't know there was a 3ft drop at the end. I mashed my nuts on the tank so hard they were like melons for a week.' After the races Pete took in Scotland and then headed for continental Europe, where he went round the Nürburgring and visited the Ferrari factory, all on the same GSX-R750WT that he'd raced. Pete Smalls, you're a typical GSX-R nutter. We salute you!

In trying to write a suitable closure for this book, I tried my best to better a comment which journalist Roland Brown told me when I was researching it. Roland has ridden every single model of GSX-R in the last decade and a half, so I will leave it to him to say:

'I owned one of the first few in the country in 1985. Suzuki put together a promotional racing package and me and the GSX-R got ourselves involved in that – to this day I still reckon it was the best bike I've ever owned or raced. You've gotta remember that proper alloy-framed barking mad supersports bikes with no centrestands and weak gearboxes just didn't exist until the GSX-R arrived! Virtually standard, it was faster than proper Formula One race bikes with tuned motors and Harris frames etc, yet it cost hardly any more than any other 750 (unlike such machines as the Yamaha OW-01 or Honda VFR750 RC30 etc). If modern bikes began with the Honda CB750 of 1969, then sports bikes began with the GSX-R in 1985, which – looking back through biking history – makes it the second most influential bike of the last century.'

History, however, has a habit of repeating itself, and this is clear when looking at the past of the GSX-R750, which from its genesis in the early 1980s and through its many evolutions over the years has found itself still at the cutting-edge of sportsbike design and still proudly wearing the GSX-R logo. It was a machine that launched a thousand race careers, countless visits to the gravel trap, a hundred acronyms, a million different suspension settings, two new breeds of motorcycle, tens of thousands of satisfied owners, and perhaps one too many psychedelic paintjobs. Here's to the next two decades of GSX-R excellence.

The GSX-R Festival – Brands Hatch

An estimated 10,000 people turned up for the GSX-R day, which was blessed with sunshine, superb track action, activities, and entertainment. Heading the bill were two and four-wheel champs Kevin Schwantz and Colin McRae, both men thrilling the crowd with their track demos. 1993 500cc GP champ Schwantz blasted around the track in a GSX-R1000 with the famous '34' sticker on it. Schwantz said: 'It's great to come back to a place like this. It's just a fun day for everybody who loves GSX-Rs. I've enjoyed the day riding the British GSX-R Superbike and the new 1,000cc race machine. It's amazing how well it handles for a new bike.' McRae was as impressive on two wheels as on four, setting times that weren't far off the racer's. He later showed how it should be done on four wheels with an impressive set of laps in a standard Ford Focus. The Clarion Suzuki GSX-R squad were also present, as were the World Superbike team. Prodigy front man Keith Flint indulged on a GSX-R600 while Suzuki's stunt man Kevin Carmichael stunned the crowd with stunt antics on board his GSX-R1000.

And even the tiddlers turned up! The rare GSX-R50. (Suzuki UK)

GSX-Rs as far as the eye can see at Brands Hatch on the day of the Festival. (Suzuki)

Appendices

1 Glossary

DAIS	Direct Air Intake System.
DOP	Dual Opposed Piston.
DPBS	Deca Piston Brake System.
Full Floater	Suzuki's rear suspension set-up.
MR-ALBOX	Multi-Rib Aluminium Box section.
NEAS	New Electrically Activated Suspension.
PAIR	Suzuki's secondary air injection system.
PDF	Positive Damping Fork.
SACS	Suzuki Advanced Cooling System.
SCAI	Suzuki Condensed Air Intake.
SCEM	Suzuki Composite Electro-chemical Material. Silicon carbide electro-plate.
SDTV	Suzuki Dual Throttle Valve.
SERT	Suzuki Endurance Race Team.
SET	Suzuki Exhaust Tuning.
Slingshot	Suzuki's carburettor set-up on the carburettors second generation GSX-R750s.
SRAD	Suzuki Ram Air Direct.
TSCC	Twin Swirl Combustion Chamber.

2 GSX-R specifications

For detailed model changes, see main Chapters.

1985 GSX-R750F

Bore x stroke: 70 x 48.7mm
Compression ratio: 10.7:1
Carburation: 4 x 29mm Mikuni
Power: 100bhp @10,500rpm
Dry weight: 176kg (388lb)
Rake/trail: 26°/107mm
Wheelbase: 1,435mm (56.5in)
Front tyre: 110/80 18
Rear tyre: 140/70 18
Top speed: 138mph (222.0kph)
Standing quarter: 11.56s/116.2mph (187.0kph)

1988 GSX-R750J

Bore x stroke: 73 x 44.7mm
Compression ratio: 10.9:1
Carburation: 4 x 36mm Mikuni
Power: 112bhp @ 11,000rpm
Dry weight: 195kg (429lb)
Rake/trail: 24.5°/99mm
Wheelbase: 1,410mm (55.5in)
Front tyre: 120/70 VR17
Rear tyre: 160/60 VR17
Top speed: 145.5mph (234.1kph)
Standing quarter: 11.54s/118.6mph (190.8kph)

Compression ratio: 10.9:1
Carburation: 4 x 38mm Mikuni
Power: 114bhp @ 11,000rpm
Dry weight: 193kg (425lb)
Rake/trail: 25.5°/100mm
Wheelbase: 1,415mm (55.7in)
Front tyre: 120/70 VR17
Rear tyre: 170/60 VR17
Top speed: 150.5mph (242.2kph)
Standing quarter: 10.87s/127mph (204.3kph)

1991 GSX-R750M
Bore x stroke: 70 x 48.7mm
Compression ratio: 10.9:1
Carburation: 4 x 38mm Mikuni
Power: 114bhp @ 11,000rpm
Dry weight: 208kg (459lb)
Rake/trail: 24.25°/100mm
Wheelbase: 1,415mm (55.7in)
Front tyre: 120/70 VR17
Rear tyre: 170/70 VR17
Top speed: 153.5mph (247.0kph)
Standing quarter: 11.3s/121mph (194.7kph)

1992 GSX-R750WN
Bore x stroke: 70 x 48.7mm
Compression ratio: 11.8:1
Carburation: 4 x 38mm Mikuni
Power: 116bhp @ 11,500rpm
Dry weight: 208kg (458lb)

1989 GSX-R750K
Bore x stroke: 73 x 44.7mm
Compression ratio: 10.9:1
Carburation: 4 x 36mm Mikuni
Power: 112bhp @ 11,000rpm
Dry weight: 195kg (429lb)
Rake/trail: 24.5°/99mm
Wheelbase: 1,410mm (55.5in)
Front tyre: 120/70 VR17
Rear tyre: 160/60 VR17
Top speed: 148mph (238.1kph)
Standing quarter: 11.5s/117.5mph (189.1kph)

1989 GSX-R750RRK
Bore x stroke: 70 x 48.7mm
Compression ratio: 10.9:1
Carburation: 4 x 40mm Mikuni flat-slides
Power: 120bhp @ 11,500rpm
Dry weight: 187kg (412lb)
Rake/trail: 24.5°/99mm
Wheelbase: 1,410mm (55.5in)
Front tyre: 130/60 VR17
Rear tyre: 170/60 VR17
Top speed: n/a
Standing quarter: n/a

1990 GSX-R750L
Bore x stroke: 70 x 48.7mm

Rake/trail: 24.3°/94mm
Wheelbase: 1,435mm (56.5in)
Front tyre: 120/70 ZR17
Rear tyre: 170/60 ZR17
Top speed: 154.7mph (248.9kph)
Standing quarter: 11.3s/122mph (196.3kph)

1996 GSX-R750WT

Bore x stroke: 72.0 x 46.0mm
Compression ratio:11.8:1
Carburation: 4 x 39mm Mikuni
Power: 122bhp @ 12,000rpm
Dry Weight: 179kg (395lb)
Rake/trail: 24°/96mm
Wheelbase: 1,400mm (55.1in)
Front tyre: 120/70 ZR-17
Rear tyre: 190/50 ZR-17
Top speed: 167mph (268.7kph)
Standing quarter: 10.7s/129mph (207.6kph)

2000 GSX-R750Y

Bore x stroke: 72 x 46mm
Compression ratio: 12.0:1
Carburation: Fuel injection system with 42mm
throttle bodies
Power: 122bhp @ 12,300rpm
Dry weight: 166kg (366lb)
Rake/trail: 24°/96mm
Wheelbase: 1,410mm (55.5in)
Front tyre: 120/70 ZR17
Rear tyre: 190/50 ZR17

Top speed: 163.4mph (262.9kph)
Standing quarter: n/a

1994 Bimota SB7

Bore x stroke: 70 x 48.7mm (749cc)
Compression ratio: 11.8:1
Carburation: TDD fuel injection
Power: 122bhp
Dry weight: 186kg (409lb)
Rake/trail: 23.5°/944mm
Wheelbase: 1,390mm (54.7in)
Front tyre: n/a
Rear tyre: n/a
Top speed: n/a
Standing quarter: n/a

1986 GSX-R1100G

Bore x stroke: 76 x 58 mm (1,052cc)
Compression ratio: 10.0:1
Carburation: 4 x 34 mm CV
Power: 130bhp @ 9,500rpm
Dry weight: 197kg (434lb)
Rake/trail: 26°/116mm
Wheelbase: 1,460mm (57.5in)
Front tyre: 110/80 18
Rear tyre: 150/70 18
Top speed: n/a
Standing quarter: n/a

1987 GSX-R1100H

Comments: Engine and chassis same as 1986
model. Colour and graphic changes only.

1988 GSX-R1100J

Bore x stroke: 76 x 58 mm (1,052cc)
Compression ratio: 10.0:1
Carburation: 34mm CV carbs
Power: 130bhp @ 9,500rpm
Dry weight: 199kg (438lb)
Rake/trail: 26°/116mm
Wheelbase: 1,460mm (57.5in)
Front tyre: 110/80 18
Rear tyre: 160/60 18
Top speed: n/a
Standing quarter: n/a
Comments: New graphics. Slightly different fuel tank. New three-spoke wheels (still 18-inch). Seven per cent bigger oil cooler. Engine and chassis same as 1987.

1989 GSX-R1100K

Bore x stroke: 78 x 59mm (1,127 cc)
Compression ratio: 10.0:1
Carburation: 4 x 36mm CV carbs
Power: 143bhp @ 9,500rpm
Dry weight: 210kg (463lb)
Rake/trail: 24.5°/99mm
Wheelbase: 1,440mm (56.7in)
Front tyre: 120/70-17
Rear tyre: 160/60-17
Top speed: n/a
Standing quarter: n/a
Comments: The second generation. New chassis, fairing, and wheels. Updated engine.

New 4-2-1-2 exhaust. Available in white/blue, black/red, and black/grey paint options. Front forks have preload, compression (8way), and rebound (10way) adjustments. Rear shock has preload and compression (4way) adjustments.

1990 GSX-R1100L

Bore x stroke: 78 x 59mm (1,127cc)
Compression ratio: 10.0:1
Carburation: 4 x 36mm CV carbs
Power: 143bhp @ 9,500rpm
Dry weight: 219kg (482lb)
Rake/trail: 24.5°/99mm
Wheelbase: 1,465mm (57.7in)
Front tyre: 130/60-17
Rear tyre: 180/55-17
Top speed: n/a
Standing quarter: n/a
Comments: New graphics, new inverted front forks. Forks and rear shock both fully adjustable. Engine same as 1989.

1991 GSX-R1100M

Bore x stroke: 78 x 59mm (1,127 cc)
Compression ratio: 10.0:1
Carburation: 4 x 40mm CV carbs
Power: 149bhp @ 10,000rpm
Dry weight: 226kg (498lb)
Rake/trail: 25.83°/91mm
Wheelbase: 1,465mm (57.7in)
Front tyre: 120/70-17

Rear tyre: 180/55-17
Top speed: n/a
Standing quarter: n/a
Comments: New fairing and graphics. New cylinder-head and carbs.

1992 GSX-R1100N
Comments: New graphics. Chassis and engine same as 1991.

1993 GSX-R1100WP
Bore x stroke: 75.5 x 60mm (1,074 cc)
Compression ratio: 11.2:1
Carburation: 4 x 40mm CV carbs
Power: 155bhp @ 10,000rpm
Dry weight: 221kg (487lb)
Rake/trail: 24.5°/100mm
Wheelbase: 1,485mm (58.5in)
Front tyre: 120/70-17
Rear tyre: 180/55-17
Top speed: n/a
Standing quarter: n/a
Comments: The third generation. New fairing. New liquid-cooled engine with lower cubic capacity. Updated chassis.

1995 GSX-R1100WS
Bore x stroke: 75.5 x 60mm
Compression ratio: 11.2:1
Carburation: 4 x 40mm Mikuni
Power: 133bhp @ 10,000rpm (restricted)
Dry weight: 221kg (486lb)

Rake/trail: 25°/100mm
Wheelbase: 1,485mm (58.5in)
Front tyre: 120/70 ZR17
Rear tyre: 180/55 ZR17
Top speed: 171mph (275.1kph)
Standing quarter: 10.07s/134mph (215.6kph)

1996 GSX-R400RR
Bore x stroke: 56 x 40.4mm
Compression ratio: 12.1:1
Carburation: 4 x 33mm Mikuni
Power: 51bhp @ 11,200rpm
Dry weight: 191kg (420lb)
Rake/trail: 25°/94mm
Wheelbase: 1,375mm (54.1in)
Front tyre: 120/60 ZR17
Rear tyre: 160/60 ZR17
Top speed: 136mph (218.8kph)
Standing quarter: 12.7s/106mph (170.6kph)

1997 GSX-R600V
Bore x stroke: 65.5 x 44.5mm
Compression ratio: 12.0:1
Carburation: 4 x Mikuni carbs
Power: 106bhp @ 12,000rpm
Dry weight: 174kg (383lb)
Rake/trail: 24°/96mm
Wheelbase: 1,390mm (54.7in)
Front tyre: 120/70 ZR17
Rear tyre: 180/70 ZR17

Top speed: 160mph (257.4kph)
Standing quarter: n/a

2001 GSX-R600

Bore x stroke: 67 x 42.5mm
Compression ratio: 12.2:1
Carburation: Electronic fuel injection
Power: 115bhp @ 13,300rpm
Dry weight: 163kg (359lb)
Rake/trail: 24°/96mm
Wheelbase: 1,400mm (55.1in)
Front tyre: 120/70 ZR17
Rear tyre: 180/55 ZR17
Top speed: 166mph (267.1kph)
Standing quarter: n/a

2001 GSX-R1000K

Bore x stroke: 73 x 59mm
Compression ratio: 12.0:1
Carburation: Electronic fuel injection 42mm
throttle bodies
Power: 161bhp @ 11,000rpm
Dry weight: 170kg
Rake/trail: 24°/96mm
Wheelbase: 1,410mm (55.5in)
Front tyre: 120/70 ZR17
Rear tyre: 190/50 ZR17
Top speed: 179mph (288.0kph)
Standing quarter: 10.39s/144mph (231.7kph)

1994 Bimota SB6

Bore x stroke: 1,074cc
Compression ratio: n/a
Carburation: Flat-slide carbs
Power: 156bhp
Dry weight: 190kg (418lb)
Rake/trail: n/a
Wheelbase: 1,390mm (54.7in)
Front tyre: n/a
Rear tyre: n/a
Top speed: n/a
Standing quarter: n/a

3 Suzuki GSX-R race results highlights

1985 Kevin Schwantz, three wins in AMA Superbike.

Mick Grant, UK *MCN* Superstock champion.

1985–6 Satoshi Tsujimoto, All-Japan TTF1 champion.

1987 Schwantz, five wins, 2nd overall in AMA Superbike.

Tsujimoto, 2nd in Daytona 200.

Yukiya Oshima, All-Japan TTF1 champion.

World Endurance champions, Herve Moineau, Bruno le Bihan, and Richard Hubin.

1988 Schwantz, Daytona 200 winner.

Doug Polen, 2nd overall in US AMA Superbike.

Scot Gray, three wins in US AMA Superbike.

Polen, US 750 Supersport champion.

World Endurance champions, Moineau and Thierry Crine.

Gary Goodfellow, World Superbike win at Sugo, Japan.

Jamie Whitham, UK Production champion.

1989 Jamie James, US AMA Superbike champion.

Scott Rusell, 2nd in US AMA Superbike championship.

Polen, All-Japan F1 (GSX-R750) and F3 (GSX-400R) champion.

Polen, World Superbike win at Sugo, Japan.

1991 Whitham, UK *MCN* TTF1 champion.

Whitham, 5th in UK Supercup.

1993 Britt Turkington, US 750 Supersport champion.

1994 Tom Kipp, US 750 Supersport champion.

1995 Fred Merkel, 2nd in US 750 Supersport championship.

1996 Aaron Yates, US 750 Supersport champion.

John Reynolds, best result of 5th, World Superbike championship, Brno.

1997 Jason Pridmore, US 750 Supersport champion.

Whitham, 3rd in World Superbike races at Hockenheim, Germany, and Monza, Italy.

World Endurance champions, Peter Goddard and Polen.

1998 Rich Alexander, US 750 Supersport champion.

Whitham, 3rd in World Superbike race at Brands Hatch, UK.

Keichi Kitigawa, World Superbike win, Sugo, Japan.

Akira Ryo, 2nd in World Superbike race at Sugo, Japan.

Ryo, 3rd in World Superbike race at Sugo, Japan.

John Crawford, British Supersport champion (GSX-R600).

Fabrizio Pirovano, World Supersport champion (GSX-R600).

1999 Karl Harris, European Superstock champion.

John Crawford, British Supersport champion (GSX-R600).

Pier-Francesco Chili, World Superbike

wins at A1-Ring, Austria, and
Hockenheim, Germany.

Ryo, World Superbike win at Sugo,
Japan.

Mat Mladin, US AMA Superbike
champion.

Stephane Chambon, World Supersport
champion (GSX-R600).

World Endurance champions, Terry
Rymer and Christian Lavielle.

2000   Chili, World Superbike win at Monza,
Italy.

Mladin, US AMA Superbike champion.

Shawn Giles, Australian Superbike
champion.

2001   John Hopkins, US Formula Extreme
champion (GSX-R1000).

Chili, World Superbike win at Donington
Park, UK.

Harris, British Supersport champion
(GSX-R600).

James Ellison, European Superstock
Champion (GSX-R1000).

Paul Young, UK Superstock champion
(GSX-R1000).

Giles, Australian Superbike champion
(GSX-R1000).

Mladin, US AMA Superbike champion.

Ryo, All-Japan Superbike champion.

Index